CONCILIUM

THE PASTORAL CARE OF
THE SICK

Edited by

Mary Collins and
David N. Power

SCM Press . London
Trinity Press International . Philadelphia

April 1991

ISBN: 0 334 03007 2
ISSN 0010 – 5236

Typeset at The Spartan Press Ltd, Lymington, Hants
Printed by Dotesios Printers Ltd, Trowbridge, Wilts

Concilium: Published February, April, June, August, October, December.

For the best and promptest service, new subscribers should apply as follows:
  US and Canadian subscribers:
Trinity Press International, 3725 Chestnut Street, Philadelphia PA 19104
Fax: 215–387–8805
  UK and other subscribers:
SCM Press, 26–30 Tottenham Road, London N1 4BZ
Fax: 071–249–3776

Existing subscribers should direct any queries about their subscriptions as above.

Subscription rates are as follows:
United States and Canada: US$59.95
United Kingdom, Europe, the rest of the world (surface): £34.95
Airmail to countries outside Europe: £44.95

Further copies of this issue and copies of most back issues of *Concilium* are available at US$12.95 (US and Canada)/£6.95 rest of the world.

Contents

Editorial

Among the revised books of the Roman Rite, that for the pastoral care of the sick deserves wider and more far-ranging exploration than it has in fact received. The book itself is of particular interest, first because it places liturgy and rite in the fuller context of pastoral action and, second, because it recognizes that a human situation needs that care and liturgy which attend to its inner diversity and its many human, social and ecclesial components.

The *Praenotanda* to the *Ordo* place the church's tradition in the care of the sick and aged within a broad human context, in which approaches to sickness vary in time with the social conditions and with the possibilities of both contemporary medicine and varied cultural healing practices. Anointing and communion to the sick are shown to belong within the pastoral care of the whole ecclesial community and a diversified prayer and liturgy. The action of the ecclesial community is then related to the attitudes to sickness and the medical practices of the surrounding society and culture.

Over the centuries some demarcations have emerged which are now subject to fresh consideration. These demarcations are between bodily health and spiritual grace, between a sickness unto death and other types of sickness, between the ministry of the baptized and the ministry of the ordained, between extreme unction and other rites or blessings touching lesser illnesses. Demarcations all too readily become dichotomies, so that any revision requires that boundaries be reconsidered. The *Ordo* does not offer definitive approaches but it invites the church to look into its traditions for a vitality that allows new attitudes and practices to develop.

This issue of *Concilium* begins with two articles that are foundational to a consideration of the pastoral care of the sick. In the first, Mary Collins surveys the content of the new *Ordo*, pointing to the different situations that it enables us to address and to the different kinds of liturgy offered. She points not only to what is said about pastoral ministry and about luturgies, but also to the implications for the life of ecclesial communities.

She likewise gives insight into the ambivalence of the *Ordo* that is inevitably characteristic of a time of transition. In the second foundational article, Patricia Maloof addresses the ways in which society looks at sickness and health. Here there is no purely individual phenomenon of personal health and psychology. Changing social conditions and different cultures offer different paradigms of health and healing, different ways in which the sick receive attention or see their own sickness. Indeed, even the forms of sickness are affected by social conditions and expectations. The church's vision and ministry fits into this varied human complex. Consequently, with these two articles we have as it were the two poles necessary for a pastoral theology and a pastoral liturgy.

The second part of the issue studies the Christian tradition itself. In combining the four articles of this section, the intention is to show the broad lines of the tradition and the diversity that has always characterized it. With more attention to non-European cultures this diversity may be even greater in the future. Dionosio Borobio traces the evolution of Christian thought and practice in early Christian centuries. In the course of his presentation he makes an important distinction and correlation between the sacrament of anointing and other parts or aspects of a healing ministry. Basilius Groen brings the practice of the Greek Orthodox Church up to date with the consideration of some very practical situations. The new *Ordo* for the Roman Rite is still very much allied with Western thought-forms. Hence it was considered opportune to offer the insights of the approach to sickness, health and healing in other cultures. Meinrad Hebga considers what is happening in the church communities of the Cameroun within the context of African culture. Adolphus Razafintsalama does the same for Madagascar. This variety of traditions invites the reader to that wider dialogue which is essential in today's global communion of churches.

There are many critical questions which remain in this field of pastoral and liturgical concern, questions whose address will be of vital importance as the Christian tradition continues to develop and to take new forms. It has been possible to address only some of them in the third part of this issue of *Concilium*. First, Meredith McGuire writes of the relation between religion, health and sickness. While religion is generally linked with healing or the capacity to sustain illness, because it is a source of coherence in the sick persons' world, McGuire is interested in how it affects the social world which is reflected in illness itself and in what religion has to say of illness. Religious beliefs and practices can have a poor as well as a beneficent influence on how illness is treated. There are also forms of illness that need to be seen as the consequence of social expectations and living conditions. The church's liturgy needs to take cognizance of this, and McGuire's article opens the possibilities of further critical attention to this aspect of ministry and belief, as well as to the socially critical role that rites can play. In the second article of this last section of the issue, David Power offers an overview of recent theological discussions about the sacrament of anointing of the sick, with specific attention to theologic-ally open questions. He suggests that these discussions are best placed within the context of the paschal and ecclesial mystery of which they are the celebration.

From many of the articles in the number it is clear that social and cultural anthropology are important to the understanding and to the development in context of the Christian tradition. However, such con-cerns are introduced in articles dealing primarily with Christian practice. By way of a different approach, in the last article in the issue Sylvia Marcos offers a specifically ethnographical study that potentially raises many issues for the church's consideration. These have to do with Christianity's relation to popular medicine, to healing rituals, and to women's mediation of health in ways that transcend the limitations of their social and cultural roles. While she does not pursue the reflection in a specifically Christian context, it is perhaps useful to close the volume with an article that presents matters for concern if Christian faith and ministry are to deepen a Christian self-understanding, enriching both its own conversation and its power for human good.

Even when all the provisions of the new *Ordo* have been considered, it is important to grasp that the present social and ecclesial situation requires great flexibility in its utilization, in keeping with the adage that sacraments are to serve people and are not a bondage on the person. Not only is the social and the medical reality subject to flux and diversity, but so are the ways in which persons belong to the church and in which they incorporate elements of Christian faith into their lives. Often enough families, faith communities and individual ministers will find themselves in positions where they want to be supportive of persons seriously impaired by sickness or old age but whose religious perspective is not of a traditional Christian mould or whose religious practice has not been that of the mainstream. They can nonetheless be helped by a personal faith and by a communion in faith that is not too rigidly defined. It is to be hoped that church members could so grasp the church's own tradition and outlook that they could creatively draw on it to serve the aged or the sick in ways appropriate to individual faith and confession in the trans-cendent.

It is important that the texts of the *Ordo* become available to all the faithful and are complemented where necessary by each culture's or each community's own perceptions. The better the tradition and the texts are known, the more adaptive and flexible people can be in aiding the sick and the aged in their approach to God and in developing their own faith in God and in Christ when faced by the enigma of human suffering.

David N. Power

No Blood for Oil. A War of Confrontation with Ourselves.

'We believe in what was sent down to us and what was sent down to you. Our God and your God is one. To him we surrender ourselves' (*Qur'an*, surah 29.46).

If Kuwait sold only orange and rice, no nation in the world would have attempted to snatch back the country from Saddam Hussein unless it had been of strategic importance. However, it can be countered, if Kuwait lived only on the proceeds of oranges or rice, Saddam Hussein would probably never have annexed it – again leaving strategic considerations aside. In *presuppositions* the opposing sides may be nearer than they would like. As early as 1980 President Carter spoke of the vital US interests in the Gulf region. So Iraq and the Allies in the Gulf War are embarking on a drama full of blood and tears.

Certainly, nothing entitles us to justify Saddam Hussein's conduct. But we know well enough from the history of Christianity that the adversaries of evil can be worse than evil itself. Paul already recognized that a self-righteous struggle for righteousness can ultimately amount to death. When the messengers of liberation with their war machines have become the messengers of hell, they no longer have any right to hold out prospects of a just world order. For the moment all we are left with is apocalyptic imagery for describing the terrors. That this war will have prevented an even worse war, even a nuclear war, cannot be either disproved or proved.

Western peace movements have summed up the problem under the slogan 'No blood for oil'. Here they touch on the real sore point, since oil has become the lifeblood of the industrialized world. By burning oil we create warmth, movement and energy. Oil has become the symbol of economic power, but also the symbol of the exploitation and pollution of the environment. Oil has led to an entanglement of capital and politics and brought about world-wide structures of dependence. Oil has become a chthonic deity. Oil gives power to the industrialized nations, but it also makes them vulnerable. No one can ordain from which holy springs oil will well up. The routes by which oil is transported are the world's arteries, around which fields of energy, characterized by anxiety and a proneness to aggression, have come into being. Since the 1970s, the long-despised guardians of the sources of oil have become lords to be hated and feared. The literary critic J. Link has drawn attention to the symbolism which has developed in Western Europe for describing first the sheikhs, then Ghadaffi and Khomeini, and finally Saddam Hussein. The symbols are those of unpredictability and madness, Hitler in a great variety of forms; those whom it depicts turn the crowds into fanatics, go around among the powder kegs with naked lights, hold their knives to our throats and threaten us with death. These projections could only come into being because the industrial nations have made their survival dependent on oil. The problem lies more in these presuppositions than in the threat itself.

For Europeans, the events came unexpectedly. The Europeans were in the process of forming a close union. This very process of reconciliation contributed towards the war; for now the UNO Security Council could speak with one voice, and thus become active for justice and peace. But as the religions have always been aware, even the UN cannot start from zero, from a state of innocence. Now Resolution 678, in its concern for peace, has legitimated war. The German Peace Movement was hit particularly hard, because out of concern for its own country it had primarily uncoupled itself from world events. Joy that non-violent revolutions are possible was followed by the realistic reading of a world which continues to be threatened by death. This war did not break in, as many people thought, like a thief in the night. With its tremendous potential for destruction it simply crystallizes and reproduces the contradictions of the present world-situation.

There is a contradiction of a world order which is organized into power centres and promises a monopolized peace. But outwardly it supports structures of violence which no one can control any longer. Monopolies of power evidently tend towards destruction. Seen in this perspective, the war was prepared by the very people who now regret it. For a decade Iraq was armed by the USSR and China, by France, England and the USA, by West and East Germany, and was used to fight against Iran's Khomeini. By fighting the terror with yet more terror, these countries pulled the whole region down into the abyss. In 1991 the Allies are fighting against their own potential for destruction. They are confronted not only with

Saddam Hussein but with themselves; the war is becoming a kind of outlet valve. At the latest after this war they will have to know what they are doing (Luke 23.34).

There is also the contradiction between the powerful lords and the helpless victims. The power-obsessed tyrant is being fought at the request of the gold-obsessed Emir. Neither Saddam Hussein nor the ruling family of Kuwait are bothered about political participation or a just social order. They have no credentials as spokesmen of their people. But the women, men and children of both states are becoming hostages to events, regardless of the degree of precision with which the bombs are dropped. No matter who wins in the end, they will remain the victims, the terrorized, the crippled, the bereaved and the dead. This contradiction has long been an argument against the morality of any war.

A third contradiction weighs even more heavily. The United Nations gave the intervention a clearly defined aim. Moreover, censored reporting has given the impression that politically the event is closely defined and geographically it is strictly limited. No one says anything about the countless losers of the war in the Third World. This war has its pitiless consequences for the North-South conflict. Who still talks about the famine in the Sahel, of the political chaos in the South Pacific, of Peru or South Africa? In June 1990 OPEC raised its oil prices by 41.7% from the level of 1 January and at the same time spoke of its unchangeable solidarity for the other countries of the Third World. There will probably be no more talk of the fund proposed at a meeting to help the developing countries. The 720 million dollars a day which the war costs, the enormous amounts of capital being destroyed every day, exclusively benefit the most perverse branch of industry there ever was – the armaments industry. This destruction of capital means poverty and death for millions of children, women and men throughout the world, for many years to come. For me that is the most morally reprehensible aspect of this war. In such a war we are killing Christ a millionfold by not doing more for the hungry and the thirsty (Matt. 25.31–40).

Fourthly, there is the contradiction between the Kuwaiti cause and the Arab cause generally. The occasion is the violation of international law, but the discussion is about the cultural spheres of the Abrahamic world religions. The historical, cultural and economic dimensions of the way in which these religions are interconnected are extremely complicated. But Saddam has presented the theme of the relationships between the religions as it is felt in the Arab world. He has declared that the war is a fight against Bush, the Satan, and the unbelievers. He has spoken of the 'mother of all battles', between right, which will conquer with the help of God, and evil, which will be destroyed by the will of God. For his part, Bush has included the soldiers and their families in his prayers and made it clear that he is the one who is fighting for the good cause. Saddam Hussein, who is not a credible representative of Islam either personally or as a political figure, has appealed to the memory and the religious identity of the Arab peoples and linked this appeal to their dreams of new greatness. It is no use arguing over the legitimacy of such dreams among people who have been deeply humiliated by a bitter colonial history. But an appeal to the affinity of the three monotheistic religions is highly significant. None of the three religions can justify this pitiless war against another religion by referring to its ethical foundations. All three religions believe in the God of love and mercy. *Shalom* and *Islam* come from the same root. Peace and justice are part of the great utopia of the hopes of these religions. That their shared monotheism has itself led to mutual suspicion is to be explained more in terms of a struggle between hostile relatives than in terms of belief in the one God. In history, Islam and Christianity were the masters of mutual oppression. For fifteen hundred years Judaism, Abraham's first religion, has been the victim of monotheistic oppression. Once again Israel is forced into the role of scapegoat.

Now at last it is finally time to work out and overcome this history together. As Hans Küng has pointed out, there can be no world peace without religious peace. The slogans of the belligerents are contradicted by all the Abrahamic religions, in the name of their own faith. The world religions, and especially the Abrahamic religions, have yet to use their potential for peace, far less transform it into politics. They all know something of human sin and guilt, the potential of human beings to destroy themselves. They all condemn inhuman power and possession which hold humanity in contempt. In all of them the question of political and social justice is alive. Finally, they all agree on one thing, that all men are children of the one God and guardians of the one earth. And they know that we are all in God's hands. Now that is an eminently political statement.

'Let the People of the Book know that they have no control over the gifts of God; that these gifts are in His hands alone, and that He vouchsafes them to whom He will. God's bounty is infinite' (surah 57.92).

Hermann Häring
Translated by John Bowden

I · Foundational Articles

The Roman Ritual: Pastoral Care and Anointing of the Sick

Mary Collins

In 1972 the Roman Congregation for Divine Worship promulgated the revised order for the pastoral care and anointing of the sick, the *Ordo unctionis infirmorum eorumque pastoralis curae*. Among the revised rites of the Roman liturgy, it has received minimal pastoral or critical attention in the past two decades and remains one of the least familiar rites of the liturgical reform.[1] This article will set out the basic structure and content of the *Ordo* and then its vision, offering theological, pastoral and liturgical commentary to draw attention to significant developments in the church's understanding of what had long been designated the sacrament of Extreme Unction, the anointing for the dying. Much that is of significance is only latent in the document and still waits to be uncovered, to be elaborated on and to be celebrated in the distinctive contexts of the local churches.

Basic structure and content of the revised *Ordo*

The *Ordo unctionis infirmorum* is a liturgical *ordo* and not simply a compendium of liturgical rites. At the least, the concept of *ordo* involves a recognition of a larger pastoral plan, within which a variety of liturgies are appropriately celebrated. The central issue for this liturgical *ordo*, according to its title, is human sickness and the many ways in which the church can be present to those who are ill. But the Introduction and the seven chapters of the *Ordo* reflect the transitional nature of the reform, since fully half of the book addresses the church's ministry to the dying.

In its pastoral plan for the care of the sick set out in the first two chapters, the church's response to illness will be the sacramental rite of anointing with the oil of the sick in some but certainly not all cases of physical deterioration or mental disorder. The Latin text describes the appropriate illness with the term *periculose*, an attempt to interpret the intent of the Vatican Council II mandate for reform of this liturgy that 'as soon as any one of the faithful begins to be in danger of death from sickness or old age, the appropriate time for the person to receive this sacrament has certainly already arrived'.[2] But the descriptive term *periculose* has itself been subject to further interpretation. The English language ritual book, confirmed by the Apostolic See, carries the note: 'The word *periculose* has been carefully studied and rendered as "seriously", rather than as "gravely", "dangerously", or "perilously". Such a rendering will serve to avoid restrictions upon the celebration of the sacrament. On the one hand, the sacrament of Anointing may and should be given to anyone whose health is seriously impaired; on the other hand, it may not be given indiscriminately to any person whose health is not seriously impaired.'[3] Debates about which clinical conditions meet such general criteria continue.[4] But what of the church's continuing ministry to the sick, prior to their sacramental anointing or subsequent to it?

Pastoral care of the sick

It is a distinctive feature of the *Ordo unctionis infirmorum eorumque pastoralis curae* that it addresses this question with utmost seriousness. It situates the particular liturgical event of the church's anointing of the sick only within the larger context of pastoral visits to the sick. During such visits ministers of the church pray with the sick and also learn directly from them; the sick are expected to offer their own testimony of their experience of the paschal mystery of Christ Jesus suffering and glorified. Words and gestures of consolation and perhaps sacramental reconciliation may be the pastoral response to the condition of the sick person. But the form and content of such pastoral visits is generally unspecified, and so leaves wide room for pastoral workers to bring the faith of the church into dialogue with the human hopes, fears and aspirations of the sick and their families. Pastoral visits to the sick provide informal opportunity for what the church knows technically as evangelization and biblical-liturgical catechesis.

During some pastoral visits, as it is appropriate, the sick are to have the opportunity to share in the local church's eucharistic communion with the risen and glorified Lord Jesus. And when and if it becomes timely, the church will again be present for prayer, for the laying on of hands, and for the anointing of the suffering person with the oil of the sick.

The scheme for the pastoral care of the sick is set out in chapters one and two of the *Ordo*. Chapter one, 'Visitation and Communion of the Sick', has two sections: 1. Visiting the Sick, and 2. Communion of the Sick. The latter section is further subdivided: Ordinary Rite and Short Rite. What is envisioned as the 'ordinary' pastoral practice for Communion for the Sick is the personal visit of the church's minister at the residence of the sick person, ideally with members of the household present. The visit is envisioned as allowing time for personal and pastoral exchange before proceeding to the liturgical action. The liturgy itself is familiarly structured on the pattern of the Liturgy of the Word and the Communion Rite of the Eucharistic Liturgy but abbreviated for the circumstances of the domestic gathering. Throughout the text, the minister is exhorted to use sound pastoral judgment and to adapt the prayer according to the condition of the sick person (OUI 40).

The most effective celebration of this ordinary Communion Rite for the Sick would seem to depend upon prior pastoral visits and ongoing household prayer. In the words of the *Ordo*, 'The sick should be encouraged to pray when they are alone or with their families, friends, or those who care for them' (OUI 44). The text gives evidence of pastoral realism when it encourages continuing formation in prayer, and directs the minister to offer this guidance. 'Their prayer should draw primarily upon the scripture, by meditating on those parts which speak of the mystery of human suffering in Christ and in his works or by using prayers drawn from the psalms and other texts' (OUI 44). When this climate of prayer has been fostered, one can imagine the possibility of honouring another directive of the *Ordo*, namely, that the sick person or other members of the household are to be involved in selecting scripture texts and prayers to be used whether in pastoral visits, in the Ordinary Rite of Communion of the Sick, or in the Rite of Anointing (OUI 45, 53, 64).

Fortunately, chapter seven of the *Ordo* provides a collection of selected scripture texts: nine readings from the Old Testament plus fourteen psalms, and forty-eight readings from the New Testament. If these are to be starting points for prayer as well as texts for ritual proclamation, they must be made readily available to the persons exhorted to use them. Given the limited access to the scriptures available to most baptized Catholics outside the Sunday assembly, and their limited familiarity with either the contents or the location of the various books of the Bible, one wonders what was in the minds of the Roman Congregation promulgating the document. Whatever they thought, the directive for continuing formation in biblical and liturgical prayer is a significant development to which we will return later.

Somewhat ironically, what is designated The Shorter Rite for Communion of the Sick, by way of contrast with The Ordinary Rite, is what has long been considered ordinary. That is the distribution of communion to the sick by a minister moving from room to room in hospitals or other institutions with only the briefest of ritual exchanges. The minister is to say the liturgical formula 'This is the Lamb of God . . . ', and the communicant is to respond with the formulaic 'Lord, I am not worthy . . .' (OUI 62). Even in the case of the Shorter Rite, however, the ritual suggests to the minister the addition of 'elements taken from the ordinary rite', as this is possible, thereby acknowledging that what is offered there is far from the pastoral or liturgical ideal (OUI 59).

The anointing of the sick
   Chapter two is entitled 'Rite of Anointing a Sick Person', and it also has subdivisions: 1. Ordinary Rite, 2. Rite of Anointing During Mass, and 3. Celebration of Anointing in a Large Congregation. The third of these forms is intended for use 'for pilgrimages or other large gatherings of a diocese, city, parish or society for the sick' (OUI 83). The prototype for this form of the liturgy is communal celebrations of the anointing of the sick which have been taking place during pilgrimages of the sick to the shrine of Lourdes in France in recent decades. In this setting, intensive public prayer of the church, regular eucharistic liturgy and eucharistic communion and occasions for sacramental reconciliation, all on a massive scale, displace the more sustained plan for the pastoral care of the sick outlined in chapter one as the prelude to sacramental anointing. While comparable massive and intensive forms for the pastoral care of the sick may exist in other dioceses and regions, they hardly constitute the normative experience of the church's liturgy for the sick. For that we must look at the first part of the chapter on the anointing of the sick.
   What is called the 'Ordinary Rite' of the anointing of the sick is a sacramental celebration in a gathering convened specifically for this liturgical action. One or more sick persons may be subjects of the anointing; one or more priests may be ministering on their behalf; one, few, or many other believers may be gathered to offer the prayer of the church with the priest and the sick. The liturgical event may take place in a sickroom, elsewhere in a household, in a church or chapel, or in another pastorally appropriate place (OUI 66,67). This form of the liturgy is 'ordinary' in distinction from a celebration of the sacrament of the anointing of the sick during the course of a Eucharistic Liturgy, the alternate option.
   The *Ordo* directs the presiding priest to plan the liturgical celebration in consultation with the sick and their families, specifically in the matter of the biblical readings and the prayers (OUI 64). This presupposes again what is envisioned in the first chapter, namely, that at least some of the

persons concerned have been formed in biblical-liturgical prayer and are ready to select texts from among those in the Rite's own lectionary in chapter seven or from elsewhere in the scripture that will be heard as good news, offering the sick consolation, hope for healing, or invitation to enter more deeply into the mystery of suffering.

The ordinary rite for the anointing of the sick, like all of the reformed rites of the Roman liturgy, has two major moments which are preceded by rites of gathering and dismissal. The first major ritual component is a Liturgy of the Word, the second the distinctive sacramental action. The crafters of this ritual clearly aimed to build upon the pastoral value of ritual familiarity. They suggest to the presider that he fashion the opening rites from among well-known liturgical units like biblical-liturgical greeting formulae, a sprinkling with holy water to signal an assembly of the baptized, a statement of the purpose of the assembly by a prayer or an exhortation incorporating the text of the letter of James, 'Is there anyone sick among you? . . . ' as a biblical warrant, and a brief penitential rite (O U I 68–71).

Once the gathering is constituted as a liturgical assembly, it proceeds to the Liturgy of the Word. In this setting what the ritual proposes is a single biblical reading. Given the breadth of the options, it is clear that what is to be proclaimed is 'the right word for the occasion', good news which can be heard as the Word of God setting the assembly free to believe, to hope, to trust, and to love. Whether or not there is to be some exposition of the scripture reading is 'dependent upon circumstances' (O U I 72). Then, in response to the biblical proclamation, those gathered move into the specific liturgical action for which they have convened.

While the sacrament is designated 'the anointing of the sick', and the anointing with holy oil is a focal moment, what is actually set out in the ritual text is a three-fold action: the prayer of the church, the laying on of hands, and the anointing of the sick person(s) with the holy oil (O U I 73–78). The liturgical action intends to replicate with simplicity the primitive ecclesial event described in the fifth chapter of the letter of James.

The 'prayer of the church' begins with one of two proposed alternatives: either a litany of intercession or a responsorial remembering of God's deeds on behalf of the sick and suffering revealed in Christ Jesus. Both forms assume that believers are gathered with the sick to support the priest's bidding with their response: 'Lord, hear our prayer' or to appropriate the priest's memorial of Jesus as one who both suffered and healed with the call for his present help: 'Lord have mercy'.

After the participatory prayer of the church on behalf of the sick, the next moment is specified with a simple ritual directive: 'The priest then lays his hands on the head of the sick person in silence '(O U I 74). What is the silent gesture about? In the liturgical tradition, the extension of hands over or on a person or a thing is a gesture of the invocation of the Holy Spirit, a ritual *epiclesis* calling for the divine Spirit to draw near and to transform the subject, making it a new creation. In the silent invocation, the church reflects its grasp of Paul's judgment, 'The Spirit too helps us in our weakness, for we do not know how to pray as we ought . . . [but God] who searches hearts knows what the Spirit means, for the Spirit intercedes for the saints as God wills' (Rom. 8.26–27).

Having first voiced its prayer on behalf of the sick and then ritually acknowledged the divine wisdom that moves it beyond words to silent prayer, the church proceeds to the anointing of the sick. The anointing itself has two moments, the first a celebration of the holy oil itself and the second the rubbing of the sick person's body with it (O U I 75a/b,76).

The reformed rite reflects a church in transition with regard to its celebration of the holy oil as a sacrament of divine presence. From the earliest witnesses to the church's use of oil for healing, it has been normative practice for the bishop to invoke divine blessing upon plant oil[5] to transform it into a healing unguent for sufferers who used it in faith. A third-century document from the Roman church, the so-called *Apostolic Tradition* of Hippolytus, specifies that the bishop invokes divine blessing on oil for the sick within the eucharistic action, just as he had moments earlier invoked divine blessing on the bread and wine of the eucharist.[6] In the early centuries, the holy oil so blessed was distributed directly to the faithful; after the eighth century priestly mediation of the holy oil for the sick was required.

The revised Roman Pontifical still presents an annual episcopal blessing of the oil of the sick as the normative practice, and indicates the significance of this liturgical blessing by setting this celebration within the solemn liturgies of Holy Week.[7] Yet new pastoral needs of diocesan churches in the twentieth century prompted the revisers of the *Ordo unctionis infirmorum* to introduce the unprecedented provision that a priest might bless the oil for the sick during the course of the liturgy of anointing (O U I 21,75). At least one practical factor influencing the change is the current provision that the sacrament of anointing might be repeated in the course of a single serious illness, something previously prohibited. A second factor is the pastoral call for a more generous use of the holy oil during the liturgical anointing. Taken together, these changed circumstances require a more ample supply of holy oil in the course of a year than might conveniently be blessed by a bishop for his diocese in the Holy Week liturgy.

Accordingly, the Ritual provides alternative texts for the ritual celebration of the holy oil itself prior to its use in the anointing of the sick person. Both a Blessing of Oil and a Prayer of Thanksgiving are offered; the first is the traditional episcopal prayer of invocation to the Holy Spirit to sanctify the oil that it may heal those who use it, and the second a trinitarian formula of praise for the salvation and healing that is mediated through the use of the oil (OUI 75a/b). In either case, the ritual book is sparse in its treatment of the celebration of the holy oil, providing nothing more than prayer texts. So ample room is given for elaboration of the celebration in its actual ritual performance, through the selection of a suitable vessel for the oil, a suitable setting for it within the liturgical space, and its handling during the prayer, whether of blessing or of thanksgiving.

The anointing of the sick with the holy oil follows immediately upon the celebration of the oil. In the revised rite a two-fold anointing with oil is called for, of the forehead and of the hands. The sobriety of the ritual at this moment is characteristically Roman, and the current revision reflects the predisposition of the Roman church to a chaste austerity in its ritual gestures. During the medieval period, when the genius of the Germanic culture dominated the Western liturgy, anointings had multiplied: eyes, ears, nostrils, mouth, head, hands, loins, feet, whatever parts of the body seemed to commend themselves for blessing. The Roman Congregation, remembering that part of the Western church's own history, accordingly made provision for more exuberant cultures. 'Depending on the culture and traditions of different people, the number of anointings and the place of anointings may be changed or increased' (OUI 24). The explicit expectation is stated that episcopal conferences will attend to this in their particular rituals.

No specification is made for the way the priest is to apply the oils; no reference is made to a cruciform action. Unfortunately reference is made to the customary use of cotton wool as a convenience to the minister in containing the oil and daubing it on the persons being anointed (OUI 22). Can one presume that what is convenient is not identical with the ideal? It is not hard to imagine a ritual anointing taking the form of rubbing the holy oil gently but thoroughly onto the skin of the sick person, in a way comparable to the application of other healing unguents. (Oily hands can be attended to easily enough; those who care daily for the seriously ill will know how to provide resourcefully for the liturgical minister.) A two-fold prayer is specified, to be prayed during the dual anointing. The text was designated by Pope Paul VI to constitute the *form* of the sacrament, according to the scholastic theological conceptualization of sacramental structure, with the holy oil as its *matter*. The prayer of anointing is quite reserved, even generic, in its call for divine aid for the sick person: 'Through this holy anointing, may the Lord in his love and mercy *help* you with the grace of the Holy Spirit. May the Lord who *frees* you from sin *save* you and *raise* you up' (OUI 76; emphasis added).[8]

Sick persons who are the subject of this ecclesial action could be forgiven for desiring greater boldness on the part of the praying church. They might well wish the church to speak with the audacity of the psalmist calling for complete restoration of health.[9] Why the 'form' is characterized by such great reserve in its expectations about physical healing is suggested in a homily of Pope Paul VI, to be considered below. But almost as though this weakness of expectation needed some correction, another prayer follows immediately (OUI 77). The priest is to choose from among one of five texts voicing a range of expectation about the sick person's transformation: from 'full health' to 'firm faith' to 'forgiveness of sin' and 'relief of pain'. The second prayer is followed by a third, the communal praying of the Lord's Prayer. It is enough to note here that such prayer texts, too, reflect a church in transition in its understanding of its own rite for the anointing of the sick, since we will take up the matter later below in discussing the vision of the rite.

The 'Ordinary Rite' of the Anointing of the Sick concludes with an expanded blessing; the ritual provides both a five-membered trinitarian or a three-membered christological pattern of invocation for blessing, healing, salvation, comfort and strength, completed each time by the 'Amen' of the gathered assembly (OUI 79). Provision is also made in the ritual text for the Anointing of the Sick for a 'mixed rite', something that is accomplished by inserting the rite for the Communion of the Sick between the Lord's Prayer and the final blessing.

The Rite of Anointing during Mass, the alternate to the Ordinary Rite, specifies that the same tripartite rite of anointing, i.e. the prayer of the church, the silent laying on of hands and the anointing of the sick with the holy oil, is to take place during the Mass at the end of the Liturgy of the Word, before the onset of the Liturgy of the Eucharist (OUI 82). Criteria are given for priests to make judgments about the selection of scriptural readings and prayer texts in this confluence of two otherwise distinct liturgical actions (OUI 81).

Pastoral care of the dying

What of the remaining chapters two through six of the *Ordo unctionis infirmorum?* At chapter three the attention of the *Ordo* shifts overtly from the care for the sick to the pastoral care for the dying. A revised rite for Viaticum, eucharistic communion for the dying, is provided.[10] Again two forms are offered, one within Mass and the other outside Mass; no designation is made about which is 'ordinary'. Either form assumes that the dying person, however weak, is conscious and able to participate actively to some degree in the prayer of the church and to receive the eucharist, whether in both kinds, in the form of bread alone, or in the form of wine alone. The suitable subject for Viaticum in the revised rite is a person in a dying condition, but one whose death is not yet imminent (OUI 26–28).

In either form, the liturgical celebration of Viaticum involves familiar opening rites and a liturgy of the Word however brief, followed by a profession of baptismal faith in the interrogatory form: 'Do you believe . . . ? I do' (OUI 108). Pastoral reality will probably dictate whether what follows is the full Eucharistic action or the rite for the Communion of the Sick. While the *Ordo* specifies the exchange of peace among the presider, the sick person and the others gathered when they are celebrating the full Eucharistic Liturgy, it omits any comparable note for the simple Communion Rite (OUI 99d). Familiar custom will un-doubtedly control what actually happens in the moments after the Lord's Prayer and before the invitation to the final communion for the dying person. In acknowledgment of that finality, the dying person is offered an additional word of blessing upon receiving the sacramental elements: 'May the Lord Jesus Christ protect you and lead you to eternal life' (OUI 112). Others receive communion in both kinds in the ordinary way. A prayer after communion and a final blessing complete the Rite of Viaticum.

Chapter four of the *Ordo Unctionis Infirmorum* is entitled 'Rite of the Sacraments for those Near Death' and subtitled 'Continuous Rite of Penance, Anointing, and Viaticum'. Chapter Five is the 'Confirmation of a Person in Danger of Death'. The continuous rite clearly reflects a pastoral situation markedly distinct from what is envisioned in the first three chapters of the *Ordo*; and it may rather reflect the contrary situation, one in which the continuing pastoral care of the sick has been neglected. But it also provides for the situation in which the onset of illness and impending death is sudden, whether caused by virulent disease or accident (OUI 30).

Priorities are set within the ritual directives for the continuous liturgical rites for the dying. For example, the priest is advised that Confirmation and Anointing ought not to be celebrated in a continuous rite, since the dual anointings can be occasion for confusion in a setting which does not allow for catechesis. Yet, a vestigial and unrepentant sacramentalism remains within the reformed rite at this point. Despite the caution, it provides for the sequence confirmation-then-anointing, 'if necessary' (OUI 117). It is unclear what would make such action 'necessary', since the ritual presumes that the dying person has already been admitted to the eucharist and will be receiving Viaticum. Sacramental reconciliation, if requested by the dying person, should precede either confirmation or anointing, however generic the confession. If time is limited, the sequence should be simply reconciliation, anointing, then Viaticum. Finally, the ritual tells the priest faced with serious strictures of time to give priority to Viaticum over the sacrament of the Anointing, since it is the former which is the sacrament of the dying, while the latter is the sacrament of the sick. However, by a curious twist reflecting once again the church's ambivalence about its own sacrament of anointing, the rite then directs that the sick [=dying?] person is still to be anointed if there is 'sufficient time' after viaticum (OUI 30).

Chapter six includes the collection of 'prayers, litanies, aspirations, psalms, and readings from scripture', which comprise the 'Rite for the Commendation of the Dying'. The collection means to ensure that the prayer of the church accompanies the dying person even after the Rite of Viaticum. The ritual ascribes responsibility for this Rite of Commendation to the ordained clergy, priests or deacons, but directs them also to prepare the laity for this ministry of prayer (OUI 142). This exhortation to the clergy to provide for the continuing formation of the laity in biblical-liturgical prayer, stated in the final section of the *Ordo* as it was in the first, raises further questions about the basic vision of the *Ordo unctionis infirmorum eorumque pastoralis curae*. It is to that question that we now turn.

The vision of the *Ordo unctionis infirmorum*

Four topics will be addressed in considering the vision of the new liturgical *ordo* for the sick: the role of the sick within the Christian community; the ministry to the sick; the catechesis needed for the implementation of the *Ordo*; and the church's ambivalence about the reform.

The sick within the Christian community
Throughout the new *Ordo*, the sick are understood to be active believers, participants in the church's ministry and its mission and also in its liturgical worship. This viewpoint is in continuity with the Vatican II Constitutions on the Church and on the Liturgy. There baptized believers are restored to their rightful place within the church and are no longer viewed as objects of the ministrations of the ordained but as agents with them of the world's salvation in Christ.

The General Introduction to the *Ordo* declares that the sick remind the rest of the church of transcendent reality, called here 'the essential or higher things' (OUI 3). Because impaired health signals human mortality, serious illness is a clear way of inviting not only the sick but also their family and neighbours to look beyond the mundane circumstances of their daily lives to consider questions of meaning. Christians no less than other humans tend to avoid facing the truth that illness, pain and death are integral to human existence. But the very presence of the sick within the community constitutes solid evidence that 'our mortal life must be redeemed through the mystery of Christ's death and resurrection' (OUI 3).

This witness to the mystery of Christian redemption is complex, involving both the sick and the larger community. The sick are called upon to fight against their own illness and to participate in their own healing. Their courage is to be complemented by their confident awareness that Christ Jesus loved the sick when others shunned them; he visited them and healed them (OUI 1). But they are also invited to contemplate the memory of Jesus pained, suffering and raised to glory through his death on the cross, and to see their own mystery reflected in his (OUI 5). The sick are understood to have access to an existential grasp of the paschal mystery and so a measure of divine wisdom unavailable elsewhere in the church.

But the sick suffer within a community of believers who are called to assist them. The redemption of human mortality must engage everyone. Health care workers provide healing skills (OUI 4,32). Associates do whatever they can to alleviate the social burdens of their illness (OUI 3,32). Family and friends pray the scriptures with them (OUI 34). And ministers of the church offer them assurance of God's gracious presence to them at a time when they are vulnerable both to self-reproach and the reproach of a God who allows their suffering (OUI 5,6). A church so engaged knows that 'sickness has meaning and value for [personal] salvation and for the salvation of the world' (OUI 1). By contrast, an ecclesial community which minimizes this mutual ministry of the sick and the healthy is likely to have little more than a shallow, notional grasp of the meaning of paschal salvation in Christ. In an era described by one cultural critic as the 'war of all against all',[11] the quiet summons of the church to attend to the sick and to learn from them is in danger of going unnoticed. But the vision of the opening paragraphs of the *Ordo* stands in prophetic judgment on the human impulse to negate the social value of the weak and suffering. Persons with seriously impaired physical or mental health, the elderly, and sick children are seen here to hold a key to the mystery of life.[12]

The ministry to the sick

The *Ordo* for the pastoral care of the sick and their sacramental anointing, as well as the care of the dying, sets out a complex ecclesial ministry. It is unimaginable that the pattern of pastoral care envisioned in this reformed liturgical book can be performed exclusively by ordained presbyters, given the shortage of priests available for the most basic work of convening the Catholic people for Sunday Eucharist. While the ritual book designates the presbyter as the 'only proper minister' of the anointing of the sick, it also acknowledges that clerical ministers need the 'assistance' of religious and laity (OUI 16,17). That understates the reality. The English-language ritual contributes to the clarification of the broadly ecclesial nature of this ministry of the pastoral care of the sick and the dying by using the more inclusive designation 'minister' in all liturgical rites at which a baptized Christian legitimately presides on behalf of the whole church: Pastoral Visits to the Sick; the Rite of Communion for the Sick; the Rite of Viaticum; the Rite for the Commendation of the Dying.[13] It may well be that the future will see added to that list the Rite of the Anointing of the Sick with the holy oil. It is certainly an inconsistency in current discipline that laity may bring the Eucharist of the church to both the sick and the dying but may not administer the oil for the sick blessed earlier in a liturgical assembly.[14]

The *Ordo* everywhere assumes that the clergy are already prepared adequately for this ministry to the sick and the dying and so are responsible for training laity to assist them. It is just as likely in many parts of the world that Catholic laity are at least as well prepared as the clergy to develop such a ministry even further. This may always have been the case. In third-century Rome, Hippolytus observed in his *Apostolic Tradition* that 'healers' (most likely those who attended the sick) did not need to be ordained because their gift was its own testimony.[15] And records of church legislation across the centuries testify to the fact that priests were regularly in need of exhortation and even sanction not to neglect the pastoral care of the sick and the dying. Invisible in this historical record is any trace of the actual pastoral care given by generations of faith-filled lay women and men before and after the priest's arrival or in his absence. The 1972 *Ordo* clearly envisions a collaborative ecclesial ministry and corporate liturgical prayer for the sick and the dying. Church office holders would do well to embrace leadership for this ministry wherever such leadership is to be found in the local churches.

Catechesis for the implementation of the Ordo

As with most ritual books, the new *Ordo* has been distributed almost universally among the clergy, but is only minimally available to the laity, even in those North Atlantic countries where books are readily available for purchase and people have money for such purchases. Ritual books are widely perceived to be clerical books rather than ecclesial ones. But for literate peoples, the ritual book itself provides a basic catechesis which can lead to new maturity of faith. Three sections of this Roman *Ordo* particularly commend themselves immediately to the adult church for its ongoing formation: the General Introduction, the Rite for the Commendation of the Dying in chapter six, and the ritual 'lectionary' found in chapter seven, that collection of scriptural texts proposed as suitable for the meditation and prayer of the sick and those who minister to them. All of these are formative of mature Christian identity, prior to and independent of their utility for a person called to actual ministry (OUI 139). They may actually serve also as an invitation to Catholics to commit themselves to prayer with the sick and the dying among their families and neighbours. The *Ordo* in fact directs that texts be made available to the laity, at least in the case of the Rite for the Commendation of the Dying (OUI 142).

While there has been much debate over what illness makes a person a suitable candidate for sacramental anointing, the *Ordo* clearly intends that adult Catholics should normally be able to judge their own condition and ask for Anointing and Viaticum, just as they present themselves for Eucharist and reconciliation (OUI 13). Effective catechesis will have to overcome the well-established bias among Roman Catholics that anointing is the sacrament for the dying. Without such reorientation of the Catholic people, clergy and lay, the new *Ordo* will be only a dead letter.

Given the vast need, little enough catechesis has occurred during homilies, even when the Sunday gospel pericopes focus on Jesus' ministry among the sick. It has been my view for some time that widespread engagement by adult parishoners in ministry to the sick is the precondition for renewed understanding of the sacrament of Anointing in the church. People who are asked to visit the sick and to pray with them out of pastoral necessity will be receiving in these encounters with the sick the evangelization on which further catechesis can build. Much attention has been directed in past decades to the way in which participation as sponsors for catechumens has brought lay Catholics to new maturity of faith. Engagement with the sick will not be less demanding for the believer. The ministry will be mutual.

Ecclesial ambivalence in a time of transition

Who among the sick should be anointed? Who should exercise the church's ministry on behalf of the sick? What do we really expect as the grace of the sacramental anointing of the sick? What ministrations does the dying Christian really need? The *Ordo* indicates that the church is not of one mind in these matters.[16] The Catholic church is a living tradition with a historical memory. Attempts to balance the continuity of its identity with the discontinuity occasioned by its historical existence are likely to generate confusion before they move toward a new integration of understanding and practice. This article has already pointed to ambivalence in the *Ordo* about quite basic questions of meaning and practice. One final question will be addressed here: what is the healing which this sacramental anointing promises?

In October 1975, Pope Paul VI preached a homily at a communal anointing of the sick during Mass in St Peter's Square. He told those who were presenting themselves for anointing that Christ's redemptive love 'intends to heal chiefly the soul yet without leaving out the body'.[17] He maintained that the Church's activity is on 'a higher, supernatural level, that of the sacraments'. His point of comparison was with the goal of medical care on the one hand and 'pseudoreligious ideas and practices that belong to the realm of superstition' on the other. The Western philosophical and theological soul-body disjunction was asserted and left unexamined. Ironically, this disjunction was also identified as 'sacramental', despite the original philosophical and theological insight that tangible earthly realities mediate invisible spiritual ones, so that health and salvation are not disjunctive. Indeed, gospel stories of Jesus's healings testify to the contrary.

Paul VI's homily incorporates conventional Western teaching on the grace of the sacrament of anointing. But insofar as the church's public worship is biblical and sacramental in its fundamental vision, theologians will have to be pressed further to clarify in what way the grace of anointing may be expected to effect personal healing without taking refuge in the body-soul disjunction. African Christians who have no cultural tradition of isolating body and soul are likely to make a unique contribution to theological development in this regard.[18] So also are all Eastern and Western practitioners of 'wholistic' medicine. Without that theological clarification, liturgical prayers emanating from the Western church will continue to be vague in any reference to renewed physical health as the expected outcome of sacramental anointing.

The church has precedence for greater boldness regarding physical healing in its prayer texts if it considers one of its sourcebooks, the prayers of the prophets and psalmist and of those who approached Jesus.

You will cure me and give me life;
My suffering will return to health.

So reads one of the most confident prayers in the book of Isaiah (38.16). The leper is equally bold in confronting Jesus: 'Sir, if you want to you can cure me' (Matt 8.3).

Reticence about praying for physical healing as an outcome of bodily anointing was certainly understandable in the centuries when physical anointing was delayed until the deathbed, and was truly extreme unction. The reticence is less understandable when the church surrounds with prayer, love, trust and faith those struggling believers whose health is seriously impaired. Both contemporary Western medicine and traditional tribal and folk medicine concur in their testimony that one's spiritual condition is a major factor in both breakdown and in healing. New subjects for this Rite of Anointing – seriously ill believers rather than dying ones – invite new attitudes in prayer. The *Ordo* is conventional rather than prophetic in this regard. But through pastoral engagement with the sick the Spirit will undoubtedly continue to teach the church how to pray.

Summary observations

One might expect, in the normal course of things, that a liturgical *ordo*, by definition a compendium of tradition, would either reflect the actual practice of the church or would lag somewhat behind ongoing developments. This book does both of those things in fair measure. But the 1972 *Ordo unctionis infirmorum eorumque pastoralis curae* also anticipates and sets direction for the church, inviting it to go beyond the familiar to embrace new practices and new attitudes in its ministry to the sick and to the dying. The result is that it is easy to use it selectively, finding in it only what one is looking for. It is also easy to criticize it where it obviously falls short of expectations. It will be a greater challenge to the local churches to use this 1972 Roman *Ordo* intelligently and to adapt it wisely.

Notes

1. *La Maison Dieu* 113 (1973) devoted a full issue to a presentation and interpretation of the 1972 *Ordo*. Extensive historical studies were done prior to the reform, among them the major work by A. Chavasse; theological studies of that era focused on the sacramental grace of anointing, especially as that had been interpreted by the Council of Trent. But recent theological-liturgical-pastoral studies on anointing are meagre, given the ubiquity of serious human illness.

2. Vatican Council II, 4 December 1963, *Sacrosanctum Concilium*, 73; OUI 8 (All references are to the *editio typica, Ordo unctionis infirmorum eorumque pastoralis curae, Typis Polyglottis Vaticanis,* 1975, since vernacular editions have often reorganized and renumbered materials for pastoral purposes. In such cases, cross references to the Latin text are normally provided).

3. *Pastoral Care of the Sick: Rite of Anointing and Viaticum*, Washington, DC: International Commission on English in the Liturgy (ICEL) 1982; note appended to paragraph 8.

4. The complexity of the social definitions of illness is explored by Meredith McGuire elsewhere in this issue.

5. In fact, Roman liturgical discipline required the use of olive oil until the 1972 reform. See the *Apostolic Constitution* 30 November 1972 that accompanied the *Ordo*.

6. B. Botte, *La Tradition Apostolique de saint Hippolyte*. Munster 1963 and 1972, no.5.

7. *Roman Pontifical*. Rite of Blessing of Oils, Rite of Consecrating the Chrism, 9–10.

8. *Apostolic Constitution*, 30 November 1972.

9. Psalm commentaries regularly treat the religious sensibility expressed in the psalms of lament of the individual, many of which give voice to the complex suffering and hope of the sick person. A number of such psalms of lament are included in OUI, ch 7.

10. Contemporary liturgical catechesis needs to be developed for the 'sacrament of Viaticum'. A start can be found in the ICEL edition of the OUI, no.175–188.

11. The phrase recurs in Christopher Lasch, *The Culture of Narcissism*, New York 1979.

12. Acknowledgement of the mentally ill as suitable subjects for the church's pastoral care and anointing is made explicit in *Pastoral Care* (ICEL), in no.53, an approved interpretation of 5 of the *editio typica*.

13. Paragraph 44 of *Pastoral Care* (ICEL) gives an explanation of this usage.

14. The 1983 Code of Canon Law, c.999.2, allows a presbyter to bless oil for the sick within the eucharistic liturgy only when the anointing will take place in the Mass. In that case, of course, the blessing will take place before and not during the eucharistic prayer.

15. Botte, *La Tradition Apostolique* (n.6), no.14.

16. David Power explores some of these conflicts and tensions elsewhere in this issue.

17. Paul VI, Homily, 5 October 1975. *Notitiae* 11 (1975), 257–58 (Italian); translated in *Documents of the Liturgy 1963–1979*, Collegeville, Mn 1982, no.3365.

18. See the article by Meinrad Hebga in this issue.

Sickness and Health in Society

Patricia Maloof

'The social character of disease is revealed by the fact that its elements consist of changes in the way people function, behave, define themselves and/or report their feelings. Deviations from the typical are what prompt people to seek medical help and to follow or reject the advice. Furthermore, such deviations serve as the basis for allowing observers (be they scientists, shamans or others) to construct what they judge to be meaningful regularities in line with sociocultural conventions, whether they are chemical, physiologic, or supernatural. These regulations become codified as disease entities and groups then certify and legitimate them' (Fabrega 1975:970).

Introduction

What is health? What is sickness? How can a person stay healthy? What causes sickness? What can be done to regain health?

Sickness and health are age-old universal conditions which elicit similar concerns and questions. However, while the concerns and questions may be the same, the responses vary considerably from one society to the next. As the quotation above clearly illustrates, social dimensions are important in defining sickness.

This article will explore how health, sickness, and healing in any society are an integral part of its cultural system. The framework for this analysis will be the health systems model, also referred to as the health care systems model, as described by Kleinman (1978). Following this will be an examination of definitions of health and sickness, aetiology, and healers and healing within a cultural framework using select examples from societies around the world.

Health and Sickness within the Cultural System – A Framework for Analysis

The health system, like other cultural systems (e.g. kinship, religious, and economic systems), is a symbolic system built out of meanings, values and behavioural norms (Kleinman 1978). In many societies, three overlapping spheres of health care can be identified: the popular sector, the folk sector and the professional sector. Each of these sectors has its way to explain and treat sickness, define who is the healer and who is the patient, and specify how the healer and patient should interact. In certain societies, the role of one sector may be minimal or have pre-eminence over the others.

The popular sector, while mostly directed towards the role of the family in recognizing and coping with illness, also includes the broader based social networks and community. It is the lay area of society where sickness is first recognized and defined, and care initiated. In addition to consultation with family, it also includes self-medication; advice from a friend, neighbour, co-worker; or healing and care activities in a church or self-help group. Interaction is informal, and the role of healer and patient may be reversed at any given time. Both share common assumptions about health and sickness and are linked by commonalities of kinship, friendship, work associations, religious membership, and so on. Understanding of this sector is particularly important for a spiritual or health-care provider because it is estimated that anywhere from seventy per cent to ninety per cent of sickness is handled within this sphere in both Western and non-Western societies (Kleinman et al. 1978:254). In other words, most illness episodes are contained within this sector, never reaching the folk or professional spheres. However, even when they do move outside the popular domain, the family provides the major context for when and where to seek care and how to evaluate the treatment.

Also of importance in this sphere is the emphasis on the maintenance of health including beliefs about the 'healthy' way to eat, drink, sleep, dress, work, play, pray – in general, how a person should live his/her life. The use of amulets or religious medallions in some societies to prevent illness is found here.

The folk arena consists of healing specialists who are not included as part of the 'official' medical system. Their forms of healing may be secular or religious in nature, or a combination of both. Examples vary from one society to another, but include a diverse group such as the health (or village) barber, midwives, bone-setters, herbalists, spiritual healers and shamans. Although this sector is large in non-Western societies, elements of it are also found in Western societies as well.

The professional sector consists of the system based upon biomedicine as well as the professionalized indigenous healing traditions (e.g. Chinese, Ayurvedic and Yunani).

Within the health system, and subsequently, each of its spheres, six core adaptive tasks are performed: 1. the cultural construction of illness as a socially learned and sanctioned experience; 2. the cultural construction of strategies and criteria to guide choices of alternative health care practices and practitioners; 3. the cognitive and communicative processes involved in the management of sickness; 4. healing activities; 5. preventive behaviour; and 6. the management of a range of therapeutic outcomes (Kleinman 1978).

This article will focus on tasks one, three and four above – definitions of health and illness, aetiology and healing – considering the relationship to cultural beliefs and practices.

Definitions of Health and Illness

As Robert Wilson (1970:12) states, 'Defining health and illness is no parochial task, and it is far from a purely theoretical exercise. What we demand as health and deprecate as disease influences our inquiries, our care, and our total sweep of social medical action.' Perceptions of health and illness vary from one culture to another and involve processes contingent upon self-perception and the evaluations of others, including family, social network, and health professionals.

The World Health Organization (1946) has defined health as the 'state of complete physical, mental, and social well-being and not merely the absence of disease, or infirmity'.

'Sickness' may in actuality refer to disease and/or illness. Fabrega (1974) has demonstrated that disease and illness are really reflecting two different perspectives. Disease connotes the biomedical model in that it involves recognition of biological and/or physiological malfunctioning. Illness refers to the experience and perception of disease within the sociocultural context. It refers to the way the individual, his family and social network recognize, explain and respond to disease. Engelhardt (1974) views disease and illness as explanatory models which reflect multiple factors and various levels of abstraction of a common phenomenon – sickness. Patient noncompliance, dissatisfaction with professional health care, and inadequate clinical care may result when 'illness' is not given the consideration it needs by the health-care provider during the course of treatment.

The concern, and fear in some cases, that sickness elicits certainly points to the high value placed upon health. Health, however it is defined or perceived, can clearly be seen as a goal. This is illustrated by such sayings as:

He who wakes up in the morning healthy in body and sound in soul and whose daily bread is assured, he is as one that possesses the world.

Ask God for forgiveness and health. After security of faith, nothing better is given to a man than good health . . .

Health is a crown on the heads of the healthy, only seen by the sick. And again: Health is an invisible luxury (Elgood 1962:51).

When studying the health and healing practices of any population, it is essential to be cognizant of its definitions of health and illness. For example, a mother may state that she would seek medical care for herself or her family when they are 'sick'; but how is this concept defined and how does a mother determine if her family is healthy or not? These definitions comprise fundamental constituents of the total system, provide information on values placed upon certain characteristics, indicate how health status is perceived, and determine what action, if any, should be taken.

This section will explore examples of definitions of health and sickness in the popular sector and go on to see how even perceptions within the professional sector may differ.

My fieldwork among various ethnic groups in the United States shows the complexity involved in a lay person's definition of health and illness. Definitions of health and illness for children and adults included three main categories: physical appearance, emotional disposition and behavioural traits. Frequently, initial responses to judging health or illness were based upon the appearance of the face and eyes and behaviour. However, keeping in mind that health and illness are relative processes, certain categories were given more or less importance depending upon the usual characteristics of the individual in question.

Case Study 1: A Sociomedical Theory of Illness

To illustrate further the importance of the sociocultural dimension in the recognition of illness, let us consider the study of the Yolngu of north-eastern Arnhem Land in Australia by Janice Reid (1986). Reid presents one of the first major studies of an Aboriginal medical system *per se* placing Yolngu ideas about sickness and death in their social context and explaining changes in these ideas in terms of the explanatory functions they serve. According to Reid, the 'sociomedical theory' of illness and death consists of a number of elements: social relationships, political relationships, and the religious life of the community (all identified as the independent variables); the values of these variables, such as hostility, peace, amity, jealousy, harmony and anger; the illness or death to be explained (identified as the dependent variable); and if applicable, any intervening variable or mechanism of causation, such as sorcery. Reid is able to explain both continuities and changes in the Yolngu medical system using this sociomedical theory. The complexity and the importance of the latter which in essence is a social paradigm is clearly demonstrated by Reid's use of hypothetical examples where the respondent was asked to identify an illness based upon symptoms that are presented and to indicate treatment. The diseases presented were pneumonia, subnutrition/dehydration, 'psychiatric illness', fatal heart attack, nephritis/cystitis, peptic ulcer, cold/flu, leprosy, and otitis media. Results show that although the Yolngu rely heavily on Western medicines and health services when sick, their theory of illness causation has changed very little in the past fifty years. The social identity and personal history of the dead person are still basic as to the cause of illness and death. Cause is indicated by the outcome of treatment rather than dictating treatment. Therefore it is not surprising when using the hypothetical examples that some of the respondents asked for more information concerning the 'patient' the researcher was talking about before they could answer.

Certainly there are other sociocultural factors that influence perceptions of health and illness. A major factor that cannot be overlooked is that of socioeconomic status. No one doubts the difficulty that people living in poverty have in responding to sickness and accessing health care. Functional definitions of health and illness are more common among poor people, probably because of their economic need to keep working and difficulty in paying for services. When daily survival is an issue, preventive health care becomes a luxury and treatment may be sought much later than is preferable. The poor often face the world with a feeling of powerlessness, where governments and bureaucracies seem to exercise the control and limit resources.

Those living in poverty often live in areas characterized by overcrowding, poor sanitation, high infant and maternal mortality rates, inadequate housing, unemployment or underemployment, malnutrition, high crime rates, minimal educational opportunities, and rarely any recreational facilities. Money, food, clothes, adequate housing, and even hope are in short supply. While urban poverty is more visible than rural poverty, issues are much the same, as are the health problems – intestinal parasites, skin infections, malnutrition, dental problems, chronic ear infections, diarrhoea and dehydration, just to name a few. For many, symptoms of the above do not become cause for concern unless the situation becomes acute. Even then, if services are availble or affordable, negotiating the system may prove to be a barrier that is difficult to overcome.

Case Study 2: The 'Green Pharmacy'

Dr Dennis Hunt, my colleague at Catholic Charities, recently returned from Brasilia, Brazil and reported on an innovative programme for health care among the rural poor. The 'green pharmacy' is based on the work of herbalists and has the collaboration of physicians who are integrating its basic concepts into training and promoting its use. A herbalist trains doctors at the local hospital as well as village repre- sentatives from outlying areas in the growing and preparation of certain herbs and their use in treatment. A small building houses consultation rooms and work areas for preparing extractions from herbs to make syrups or teas and to dry herbs. Physicians and social workers are actively involved, serving as diagnosticians and consultants. While 'Western' medicines are prescribed in certain acute cases, the use of herbal medicines is encouraged in other instances. Villagers are given 'starter sets' and are trained how to grow and use the plants for various ailments. The 'starter set' consists of about twelve plants that have been tested for toxicity to ensure that overuse or misuse will not cause any harmful consequences. Such a programme serves two important purposes: 1. the rural poor have access to affordable treatment, thus receiving relief of symptoms; and 2. individuals become empowered to take more control over their own lives even without money.

While the complexity of definitions of health and illness within the popular sector and, following from these, if or when to seek care may not be surprising, it is also possible to document differences within what would seem to be one system – 'Western' medicine – based upon a biomedical model and the views of the professional sector. It too does not exist in a sociocultural vacuum. Ultimately, it too expresses the values of the societies in which it exists and reflects the inequalities and hierachies reminiscent of the society at large. Helman (1990:63–8) concisely summarizes various studies on how doctors reflect the underlying cultural values of their societies (US and European) and how this determines the diagnosis and treatment of sickness. For example, he quotes a study in 1984 which compared the twenty leading diagnostic categories and the twenty leading types of drugs prescribed in five countries (the UK, Germany, Italy, France and Spain). Disparities in the health of the populations apparently were not sufficient to explain the marked variations. The major group of drugs prescribed in the UK were tranquillizers, hypnotics and sedatives, accounting for 8.6% of the total number of prescriptions, compared with 6.8% in France, 6.0% in Germany, 3.1% in Italy and 2.0% in Spain. 'Neuroses' were common diagnoses for the UK (5.1%) compared with 4.1% in France, 3.2% in Italy and 1.7% in Spain. Differences have also been noted in the diagnosis of schizophrenia and affective disorders between psychiatrists in the US and the UK as well as differences in the rate of surgical procedures between the US and other countries. Cultural values are thus seen to be reflected even in the biomedical model when it comes to treating and diagnozing disease.

Aetiology

Within any sphere of the health system – be it popular, folk or professional – a patient (and his family and social network) and a health-care provider label, classify, and explain the sickness episode in such a way that it is personally and socially meaningful. These explanations or explanatory models (EMs) can be used to explain aetiology, onset of symptoms, pathophysiology, course of sickness (both severity and type of sick role) and treatment. Frequently, a patient will not fully discuss his explanatory model, which may tend to be less abstract and possibly appear to be inconsistent or self-contradictory to the health-care provider. Nevertheless, EMs are attempts to explain illness just as health-care providers use the biomedical model to explain disease. When the models between patient and practitioner conflict, then impediments to health care arise which may affect the patient's compliance, satisfaction and effective use of health-care services. The EM of a patient is influenced by numerous factors such as cultural beliefs (including definitions of health and illness, cultural explanations of anatomy and physiology, etc.), socioeconomic status, education, occupation, religion, and past experiences with illness and health care. The patient may combine or blend the differing models and thus hold more than one explanation for an illness. This author has observed such occurrences on numerous occasions. In fact, multiple causation of illness is a well-known phenomenon, but some causes may be given more emphasis than others by the patient and may include what are commonly termed 'folk beliefs' or 'popular aetiology'. EMs are attempts to give some order and meaning to events by relating them to a particular culture's underlying conception of the universe and what it judges to be reality. With many popular or folk aetiologies, human relations are regarded as the most basic of all realities, and as a result the EM may reflect a subjective and personalized outlook – i.e. illness and death are related to problems in interpersonal relationships as well as to such negative characteristics as envy, spite, anger, etc. Biomedicine, on the other hand, is seen to be objective, impersonal and based upon physiological processes, thus providing little personal and social meaning to the illness experience.

This section will not discuss aetiology as explained by the biomedical model – e.g. germ theory of disease, contagion, physiological basis, and so on. Instead, emphasis will be placed upon three other concepts which are central to understanding sickness in much of the popular and folk healthcare sectors throughout the world. These are: 1. a holistic approach to health and illness without a mind-body dualism; 2. humoral theory; and 3. the evil eye. Each of these will be illustrated by a case study.

Before beginning this discussion, it is imperative to state that concepts of aetiology and healing around the world often involve the supernatural, either explicitly, or implicitly. 'Religion', however it is defined, is an integral part of the cultural system, and for many societies it sets the code by which one conducts one's life. With societies that value the separation of 'church' and state, people learn to compartmentalize their lives and keep their religious beliefs within a private domain. Values arising from these beliefs are still operative on a daily basis, but not necessarily in a very visible manner.

For other societies no such dichotomy exists either in the public or private domain. Referring back to Yolngu society, Reid (1986:XXV) makes this point when she states, 'To query the existence of the central idea of sorcery and all that it represents would be to query the myriad links between human behaviour, social order, ritual practice, and spiritual well-being – the complex of relationships on which, in Yolngu eyes, the continuity of their society depends' (p. xxv).

This oneness of religious beliefs with the totality of a person's life is further illustrated by one of my students who wrote that, 'Religion is more than the box you check on a form, religion is like the air you breathe.'

One last quotation to emphasize this point is a statement given by Kay (1978:7):

However, one person's religion is another's magic, witchcraft, or superstition. Traditionally, a fascination of anthropologists and folkorists, the study of religion, magic, and witchcraft is difficult for health professionals to see as directly relevant to their practice. It is equally difficult for them to realize that for some groups religion is an equivalent of science.

Returning to lay theories of aetiology in general, Helman (1990:102–113) lists four sites of origin: 1. within the individual; 2. in the natural world; 3. in the social world; and 4. in the supernatural world. None of these are mutually exclusive since lay theories of illness aetiologies are often multicausal. This will be further illustrated by the three examples discussed below which relate to more than one of the above at the same time.

For the diagnosis of disease in the biomedical model there has been an increasing reliance on technology and defining parameters of health and illness numerically as test results relate to what are seen as 'normal' ranges. While some sectors of the medical profession approach disease from a holistic perspective, physical and biochemical measures remain the rule. 'Physical' health or disease therefore is seen as an objective identification of physical changes in the function or structure of the body. 'Disease' (e.g. hepatitis or tuberculosis), no matter what society it appears in, is to have basically the same clinical picture – i.e. similar form, symptoms, process, and treatment. Within this framework, little allowance is made for the social and psychological process. This perspective strongly expresses the mind-body dualism often identified with so-called 'Western' medicine. Some scholars, tracing back to Descartes in the seventeenth century, find evidence of the origin of this theory. 'Man' was divided into 'body' which was studied by scientists, while philosophers and theologians studied the 'mind' or 'soul'. Today, psychiatrists and behavioural scientists are the specialists concerning the mind while other medical scientists take care of the physical body with an emphasis on technology to aid in diagnosis. However, while it may be common to speak of 'physical' and 'mental' health and illness in the professional sector, in actuality, many people around the world view health, illness and their bodies in a more holistic sense as a system. In addition, this system also includes a spiritual component. Thus, all three parts of the individual – mind, physical body and soul – are united as one. Distress in any of these three parts may contribute to 'dis-ease' (or 'illness') in any other part. Coming from this, a patient may express emotional difficulties through physical symptoms (i.e. somatization), and a healthy mind and soul may be seen as important components to a healthy body. In actuality, then, the patient perceives these three components as a 'unity'.

To illustrate this point, the reader may want to consider the case of a client who complained to me about how her doctor 'had not helped' her. Yes, the presenting physical symptoms were gone, but the patient was still not 'cured'. The author suggests that attention to this patient's physical complaints was only one part of her illness and her other needs had not been met.

In the literature, there is often reference to what have been termed 'folk illnesses'. These are 'syndromes from which members of a particular group claim to suffer and for which their culture provides an etiology, a diagnosis, preventive measures, and regimens of healing' (Rubel 1977). More than just symptoms, these illnesses also have symbolic meanings for the members of the society in a moral, social or psychological sense. Illnesses may be seen to reflect supernatural forces, changes in the environment, or social conflicts, but be manifested in physical symptoms as a way to better deal with the issues in a socially appropriate manner. It is a way to restore harmony within oneself and with others without open confrontation. Examples include *susto* in Latin America, *amok* in Malaysia, and *narahatiye qalb* in Iran. Numerous other examples can be found throughout the world.

Case Study 3: 'Heart Distress'

While in Iran I witnessed what has been documented by Good (1977) as 'heart distress' (*narahative qalb*). The heart is described with such physical symptoms as 'trembling', 'fluttering' or 'pounding' and accompanied by feelings of anxiety, sadness or anger. It is more common among women, although I also observed it among men. 'Heart distress' can be seen as reflective of the conflicts in a patient's life and was observed by Good frequently to follow quarrels within the family, infertility, use of contraception, pregnancy, childbirth or death of a close family member. While a patient may not readily be able to express her discomfort over these issues, particularly in an extended family situation, or divulge family relations to an outsider, to complain of symptoms related to the heart is culturally acceptable and the patient receives the kind of emotional support she needs, if not some physical relief. Thus, this one illness encompasses and symbolizes physical, psychological and social difficulties.

Humoral theory is another common folk aetiology and closely related to the tripartite system as expressed above. In extremely simplistic terms, without discussion in this article of its development or divergent forms, humoral theory refers to maintaining a balance of the various elements of the body so that the system is kept in equilibrium. The most common expression of this theory today is seen by efforts to maintain a balance between 'hot' and 'cold' in the body. 'Hot' and 'cold' do not refer to temperature as measured by a thermometer, but rather to the intrinsic nature of things. 'Hot' illnesses are treated with 'cold' foods, herbs, and medicines to restore the balance. The same principle is followed for 'cold' illnesses by treating them with 'hot' remedies. Interpretations as to whether a particular food, medicine, or even cooking method is regarded as 'hot' or 'cold' varies from one part of the world to another. Nevertheless, the basic principle of harmony or balance is the same and this interpretation of aetiology has implications for the professional sector.

Case Study 4: Humoral Theory

Mull and Mull (1988) report on the difficulty in gaining acceptance for oral rehydration therapy (ORT) in rural Pakistan. Despite its promotion by the government and free availability some mothers did not accept its use for diarrhoea. First of all, the latter was not always recognized as a disease, but as a 'natural part' of teething and growing up. Some blamed the evil eye or malevolent spirits for the diarrhoea, in which case treatment was sought through traditional healers or remedies. Since diarrhoea was viewed as a 'hot' illness, then to stop it would trap the heat in the body and cause a fever. To treat a 'hot' illness, a 'cold' form of treatment is needed. For an infant with diarrhoea, this would usually take the form of a change in the maternal diet or giving certain herbs or foods to the infant. Since most Western medicines are seen as 'hot', then they would not be viewed as appropriate for this illness. Thus the ORT, classified as a 'hot' medicine, was then rejected by some of the mothers.

The documentation of the beliefs concerning the relationship of the supernatural to health and illness around the world is monumental. From soul loss to spirit intrusion, as punishment for omission or commission of acts by oneself or one's ancestors, as the work of malevolent spirits and so on – the examples are numerous. A common belief, found in 36% of the world's population, is that of the evil eye (Bernardo 1981).

Case Study 5: The Evil Eye

The concept of the evil eye is defined for our purposes as the power of certain individuals, whether voluntary or involuntary, to cast a spell or to produce a malignant effect upon animate or inanimate objects upon which their eye may fall. Belief in the evil eye predates Islam, Christianity, Judaism, and Zoroastrianism in the Middle East, its core area. However, belief in the evil eye is also found throughout the Mediterranean, South Asia, northern Europe, North Africa, along a sub-Sahara fringe into parts of East Africa, and in Latin and South America. Depending upon the area of the world, it is believed to cause any type of misfortune. The most vulnerable to its attack are children.

An example recounted to me by an Arabic-speaking woman in the US clearly demonstrates the strength of this belief. The respondent was a thirty-six year old woman who had been in the United States for nineteen years at the time of the interview. She told of the time she had taken her child to the doctor for a well-baby check-up. The doctor said the child was fine and healthy, so she left and took the baby to visit at a friend's house. At the time, the respondent was still nursing her baby. The friend commented on how beautiful the baby was and said, 'I see your milk in his face.' Later that day, when they were home, the baby became ill: his neck became stiff and swollen, but he had no fever. Taking him back to the doctor the next day, the respondent stated that the baby was found to have a 'cyst' and it was removed by the doctor. The mother told the researcher, 'He had an eye there (pointing to the afflicted area) and since that time I put a cross around his neck.'

In the case described above, the explanatory model of the patient differed from that of the physician, but the latter, as part of the professional sector, was sought out for a cure which was supplemented by other remedies for the evil eye at home. In other situations, such a blend of traditional beliefs and/or practices may not blend as readily as was noted in the example of ORT in Pakistan.

Healers and healing

Given the complexity involved in defining health and illness and in the determination of aetiology it follows that healing techniques and types of healers are numerous. While the emphasis in the professional sector is on a dyadic relationship such as physician-patient, other societies actually have a multiperson network of care-providers including family, social network, and non-relatives. However, in any society, a plurality of health caregivers exists. For the UK, Helman (1990:83) lists thirty-six major types of healers from the professional, folk and popular sectors combined, including some with a spiritual basis. Many of these major categories also have sub-groups as shown below:

Professional, folk and popular healers in the UK

Hospital doctors (NHS)
General practitioners (NHS)
Private doctors (hospital or GP)
Nurses (hospital, school, and community)
Midwives
Health visitors
Social workers
Physiotherapists
Occupational therapists
Pharmacists
Dieticians
Opticians
Dentists
Hospital technicians
Nursing auxiliaries
Medical receptionists
Local authority health clinics
Clinical psychologists and psychoanalysts
Counsellors (marriage, child-guidance, pregnancy, contraception)
Alternative psychotherapists (gestalt, primal therapy, etc.)
Group therapists
Samaritans and other phone-in counsellors
Self-help groups
Yoga and meditation groups
Health-food shops' salespeople
Media healers (advice columnists in newspapers and magazines, TV and radio doctors)
Ethnic minority healers
    Muslim hakims
    Hindu vaids

Chinese acupuncturists and herbalists
West Indian healing churches
Healing churches and cults
Christian healing guilds
Church counselling services
Hospital and other chaplains
Probation officers
Citizens' Advice Bureaux
Alternative healers (lay and medical)
    Acupuncture
    Homeopathy
    Osteopathy
    Chiropractic
    Radionics
    Herbalism
    Spiritual healing
    Hypnotherapy
    Naturopathy
    Massage
    etc.
Diviners
    Astrologers
    Tarot readers
    Clairvoyants
    Clairaudientes
    Mediums
    Psychic consultants
    Palmists
    Fortune tellers
    etc.
Lay health advisers (family, friends, neighbours, acquaintances, voluntary or charitable workers, salespeople, hairdressers, etc.)

Bannerman, Burton and Wen-Chieh (1983:11), editors of a volume on traditional medicine for the World Health Organization, state that approximately half of the world's population live in countries which have departments or ministries responsible for traditional medicine. In addition, eighty per cent or more of the rural populations in many countries are cared for by traditional practitioners and birth attendants. As pluralism in health care extends throughout the world, it is important to facilitate the interaction between biomedical and traditional health-care practitioners and practices. In cases where behavioural, emotional and spiritual factors play an important role, treatment of physical symptoms is insufficient. I recall the case of an adolescent male who was brought to the attention of a 'refugee centre' which did not provide mental health services. It was a late Friday afternoon, difficult to reach anyone who was capable of assessing him in his mother tongue, and concern existed as to whether this youth were suicidal. Until appropriate care could be located, the youth was taken to the local Buddhist temple where he spent the weekend. The monk counselled him and obtained a promise from the youth that he would not commit suicide. Such a promise given to a monk is a solemn oath, and the refugee workers knew that they had gained a bit of time in locating appropriate services.

I have also seen refugee mental health centres in the United States that have a Buddhist monk on staff. In many ways, this role is similar to what is more commonly referred to as pastoral counselling. However, traditional medicine is effective in treating more than just psychosomatic illnesses, since it also has a solid foundation in using herbs in the healing of organically based illness.

Case Study 6: Traditional Medicine Centres

Hiegel and Landrac (1990) report on the use of traditional medicine centres (TMCs) in refugee camps in Thailand beginning more than ten years ago. These centres are linked with the camp clinics and hospitals, but operate independently. A *kru*, traditional healer, may treat the patient with traditional methods or refer him/her to another physician in the camp. In some of the camps, the *krus* from the TMCs also make daily rounds in the hospitals. Patients thus feel more at ease in the hospital by being able to receive both forms of treatment.

A good example of how traditional practices complemented Western medicine in the camps is illustrated by the encouraging of fluid intake of Kampuchean nursing mothers. Some mothers insisted that they did not have enough breast milk to feed their babies and therefore preferred to bottle feed. They were told to drink more water, but few heeded this advice. However, traditionally, nursing women drink large quantities of a liquid of boiled herbs which are thought to increase the quantity and quality of the mother's milk. Once a large quantity of this medication was prepared every day and made available throughout the camp, even in the hospital, women began drinking litres of it, whereas they had not been drinking water.

Case Study 7: A Healing Centre

Young, Ingram and Swartz (1988) report on a Cree healer from northern Alberta, Canada. He has decided to develop a healing centre on his reserve for the treatment of native and non-native patients. This centre will 'allow him to combine a modern facility with traditional treatment procedures' (p.40). A receptionist would greet patients, make appointments, and direct patients to a private room for treatment by a healer. Each healer would be a specialist (e.g. chronic diseases, contagious diseases, alcohol abuse, etc.), providing treatment along traditional lines, with each operating a sweat lodge and administering herbal medicines.

Who is a healer? How does a healer heal? Again, universal questions with a multitude of answers. But world-wide, it is possible to see that healing occurs on three levels: physical, emotional and spiritual. Cross-cultural studies have shown much more flexibility in therapeutic choices than in medical beliefs, which are less readily abandoned.

Conclusion

It is rare in any society to find people who are able to accept incapacitating illness, injury, or death as caprices of nature and not question why they or members of their families should be afflicted. Human beings abhor inexplicable suffering. In order to explain and cope with serious misfortune, each society has evolved sets of ideas and practices which can be invoked to explain the cause of an illness or death and help cope with its ramifications. (Reid 1986:32).

Considering sickness and health in society world-wide, this article has demonstrated a pluralism of beliefs and practices as well as the integration of different sectors of health care (popular, folk and professional). The focus has been on individuals, but it is possible to extend the metaphor of sickness to society as a whole. Looking at such issues as crime, substance abuse, child abuse, violence against women, hunger, homelessness and war – to name a few – it is possible to see how all of these are sicknesses at a societal level. All need various forms of healing, and once again three aspects must be addressed: physical, emotional and spiritual.

Bibliography

R. Bannerman, J. Burton and C. Wen-Chieh, *Traditional Medicine and Health Care Coverage*, Geneva 1983.

S. Bernado, *The Ethnic Almanic*, Garden City, NY 1981.

C. Elgood, 'Tibb-ul-Nabbi or Medicine of the Prophet', *Osiris* 14, 1962.

H.T. Engelhardt Jr, 'Explanatory Models in Medicine', *Texas Reports on Biology and Medicine* 32, 1974, 225.

H. Fabrega Jr, *Disease and Social Behavior*, Cambridge, Mass. 1974.

H. Febrega Jr, 'The Need for an Ethnomedical Science', *Science* 1989 (1975), 969–75 (Sept. 19).

B. Good, 'The Heart of What's the Matter: The Semantics of Illness in Iran', *Cult. Med. Psychiatry* 1, 1977, 25–58.

J-P. Hiegel and C. Landrac, 'Two Types of Healing', *Refugees* 74, 1990, 26–8 (April).

C. Helman, *Culture, Health and Illness*, London 1990.

M. Kay, 'Clinical Anthropology', *The Anthropology of Health*, ed. E.E. Bauwens, St Louis 1978.

A. Kleinman, 'Concepts and a Model for the Comparison of Medical Systems as Cultural Systems', *Social Science and Medicines* 12 (2B), 1978, 85–93.

A. Kleinman, L. Eisenberg and B. Good, 'Culture Illness and Care: Clinical Lessons from Anthropological and Cross-Cultural Research', *Annals of Internal Medicine* 88, 1978, 251–8.

J.D. Mull and D.S. Mull, 'Mothers' Concept of Childhood Diarrhea in Rural Pakistan: What ORT Program Planners Should Know', *Social Science and Medicine* 27, 1988, 53–67.

J. Reid, *Sorcerers and Healing Spirits*, Elmsford, NY 1986.

A.J. Rubel, 'The epidemiology of a Folk Illness: Susto in Hispanic America', *Culture, Disease, and Healing: Studies in Medical Anthropology*, ed. D. Landy, New York 1977, 119–28.

R. Wilson, *The Sociology of Health: An Introduction*, New York 1970.

World Health Organization, *Constitution of the World Health Organization*, Geneva 1946.

D. Young, G. Ingram and I. Swartz, 'The Persistence of Traditional Medicine in the Modern World', *Cultural Survival Quarterly* 12, 1988, 39–41.

II · Varieties of Christian Tradition

An Enquiry into Healing Anointing in the Early Church

Dionisio Borobio

The most effective historical enquiries are those that lead to the most coherent practical renewal, and this is the guiding principle of this article. Its basic aim is to show the healing significance and purpose which the early church (of New Testament times and the first centuries, that is) accorded especially to anointing. This occupied a privileged position, both for understanding the charisms of healing, and in the exercise of these charisms through different rites and healing practices.

The sources for such a study, naturally, have to be the New Testament and the patristic and liturgical testimonies of the period,[1] of which only a synthesis of comparison and conclusion can be presented here. The hermeneutical context of this study needs to be situated in the period and cultural ethos of the time, when links between sickness and the sources of evil and of sin and punishment, and so of exorcisms and magical healing rites, were commonplace; when the evolution of medicine was at a very basic and rudimentary stage, and so means of healing were based more on nature and superstition than on technology; and when the question asked of sickness was therefore not so much 'What?' or 'How?', as a religious 'Why?'.[2]

For the sake of clarity, I have divided this study into three parts, the subject-matter of which inevitably overlaps: 1. charisms of healing; 2. rites of healing; 3. practices of healing.

1. Charisms of healing

The 'charism of healing' is that lasting and extraordinary gift which some people receive from God, practised in various circumstances and special situations. This charism is not necessarily linked to, and should not be confused with, the sacrament of anointing of the sick. In itself, it is not tied to a set formula, nor to a particular rite, nor to a specific group of persons. It depends on the sovereign and free action of the Spirit (I Cor. 12.11).

Looking at where these charisms of healing appear in the New Testament, we find that Jesus is the first great Healer, possessing the charism of healing in a unique, unrepeatable and wonderful way, and using it to fulfil the messianic promises of liberation (Isa. 35.5–6; 61.1–3; Jer. 33.6; Matt. 11.3–6; Luke 4.21). His healing is at once bodily and spiritual, integral and of the whole person (see Mark 2.1–12: the cure of a paralytic; John 9.1–45: the cure of a man blind from birth). Jesus takes up and carries to completion the prophetic healing function proclaimed in the Old Testament (Elijah, Elisha, see Matt. 12.3–6), not only curing sicknesses, but above all healing the whole person (Matt. 4.32) from all pain and sorrow, from all injustice and abandonment, from all slavery and sin: 'He took our sicknesses away and carried our diseases for us' (Matt. 8.17, quoting Isa. 53.4). This makes his healings not a matter of showing off healing powers, but the definitive proof of the presence of the kingdom in the true liberator messiah, evidence of a unique 'charismatic possession' (anointing) by the Spirit (Luke 4.16–27; Matt. 12.9–32).[3]

Jesus communicated and transmitted this 'charism' and ministry of healing to the apostles in two stages and as complementary 'bequests': on the first mission, during his earthly life: 'They cast out many devils, and anointed many sick people with oil and cured them' (Mark 6.13); and on the second mission, after his Pasch: 'Go out to the whole world; proclaim the Good News to all creation . . . These are the signs that will be associated with believers: in my name they will cast out devils; they will have the gift of tongues . . . they will lay their hands on the sick, who will recover' (Mark 16.15–17). The charism of healing should be understood as forming part of and an integral element in the overall mission. This is an 'unequal' but true, at once historical and prophetic, anamnetic and charismatic, mission and continuation of Christ's complete ministry to the sick. Jesus did not tell the apostles to carry out anointings, but to continue his work among the sick. The mission in Galilee was an anticipation of the paschal mission, which they could carry out only in the power of the Spirit (see John 20.21–23).[4]

The texts show that in fact this continuation was effected in three forms in the early community: an ordinary form, through the gifts and services of healing (I Cor. 12.7–9, 28–30; Acts 6.1–2; II Cor. 1.5–6; Col. 1.24); an extraordinary form, through cures (Acts 3.1–26); and a 'sacramental' form, through prayer and anointing (James 5.13–16). To take the extraordinary charismatic continuation: this seems to be clearly attested both by rabbinical writings which reject such behaviour on the part of Christians,[5] and by the Acts of the Apostles, which witnesses to it with approbation (see 2.43; 5.12, 15–16; 8.7; 9.12–17.34; 28.8ff). For the early community, these miraculous cures were always carried out in the name of the Lord Jesus and by the power of his Spirit (Acts 3.6–7); they are a repetition, by which he is made present, of those Jesus carried out during his earthly life; they even repeat the same sequences and chain of reactions: curing, crisis, accusations, faith (Acts 3).

The numerous accounts of exorcisms, cures and marvellous interventions found in early witnesses by church historians or in lives of the saints[6] – given the logical 'inequality' and critical interpretation these must be accorded – also belong in this line of extraordinary charismatic continuation. It is difficult to separate out the dose of magic, superstition and legend these tales from the past may contain – as it is with so many present-day happenings. It is impossible for us to tell how far human nature or psychology extends, or what can be unleashed from the hidden stores of nature, and where the realm of the extraordinary, the supernatural and the miraculous begins. We have no exact science for infallibly determining the where, how and when of God's extraordinary intervention through the actions of those who possess these charisms of healing. One thing is certain, however: given the importance this charism had in Christ, it is totally coherent, and even 'required', for it to form an integral part, too, of the continuation of the church's ministry to the sick.[7]

2. The rites of healing

Although various witnesses speak of different rites of healing, the most important one they refer to is undoubtedly anointing with oil. Bearing in mind the meaning, application and lifegiving-healing-purifying power attributed to oil in the scriptures,[8] and also in the early church, the following elements are worth examining.

(a) In the New Testament

Jesus' preferred gesture of healing seems to have been the laying-on of hands: 'At sunset all those who had friends suffering from diseases of one kind or another brought them to him, and laying hands on each he cured them' (Luke 4.40; see Mark 1.40–41; 5.22–23, 41). Sometimes this laying-on of hands extended to special contact with the organ that was diseased: eyes, tongue, for example (Mark 8.22–26; John 9.6–7; Mark 7.32–36).

Though exclusively physical healing is not the intention in every case where anointing with oil is mentioned, its use nevertheless merits special attention. Mark clearly establishes a direct connection between the rite of anointing with oil and healing the sick, within a broader religious and evangelizing context, which supposes a call to conversion and liberation from all evil and the power of the devil: 'So they set off to preach repentance; and they cast out many devils, and anointed many sick people with oil and cured them' (6.13). But the connection is not exclusively with anointing with oil: after the resurrection, Mark extends also it to the laying-on of hands: 'They will lay their hands on the sick, who will recover' (16.18). Both rites, anointing with oil and laying-on of hands, appear to have the same function and therapeutic-healing signifying power, within a context of mission and liberative evangelization. Although anointing manifests the healing aspect more clearly, whereas the laying-on of hands better expresses the origin and authority (Christ) of the healing power, the two rites are complementary and point in the same direction.[9]

This connection between anointing and healing also appears in James 5.13–16: ' . . . they must anoint him with oil in the name of the Lord and pray over him. The prayer of faith will save the sick man (*sosei tou kamnonta*) and the Lord will raise him up again (*egerei auton*)'. This is not the place for a detailed exegesis of this passage, which has already been made by more competent authorities.[10] Here I just wish to stress the aspect that concerns us. It seems clear that James, too, is establishing a link between the rite of anointing and the effect of healing; this is implied by the verbs he uses (*sosei, egerei*) in view of their usual meaning in the whole biblical tradition. The fact that these verbs also carry an eschatological meaning of salvation (eternal life or salvation, resurrection) is not in conflict with their physical meaning of healing. In the closest line of continuity with Christ's ministry to the sick, they must refer to an integral physical-spiritual, present-eschatological, healing or saving. The effect of 'saving and strengthening the sick' is not reductive but extensive, not partial but total. Coherent continuity with Christ's ministry to the sick, the Hebrew people's anthropological and biblical conception, comparison with other texts and places, the relationship between temporal and eschatological health, the very fact that our text implies an 'open' interpretation . . . all justify this conclusion. Besides, the power of healing is the temporal exercise of a power of resurrection, which refers to the final resurrection (see Luke 10.20).

(b) In patristic texts

From the earliest times, anointing appears to have had a plurality of uses, but its preferred use is for the healing of the sick. So Irenaeus speaks of oil that is poured on the head of the dead.[11] Origen refers to anointing as one of the forms of forgiving sins.[12] Aphraates (fourth century) describes its multiple use in these terms: 'Oil is the symbol of the sacrament of life which perfects Christians, priests and kings; it lightens the darkness, anoints the sick and reintroduces penitents.'[13] The *Egyptian Constitutions* (fifth century), amplifying the *Apostolic Tradition* of Hippolytus, say much the same: 'As by sanctifying this oil you give health to those who use and taste it, and thus you anointed kings, priests and prophets, so in the same way this oil brings comfort to those who taste it, and health to those who use it.'[14] Pseudo-Dionysius was also to speak in the same manner of the different uses of oil: 'Then the bishop pours out the oil on the dead person. In speaking of baptism I have already explained how the initiate was first anointed with oil . . . in the first place he who is going into battle is anointed at the outset, and then when all battles have ceased he who no longer faces them is also anointed.'[15] These texts show that the use of oil in the early church was polyvalent and diversified according to different situations in life, from its beginning to its end. Its most common significance was consecration, sanctification, fortifying.

Its principal usage was that made for the purpose of healing, by virtue not only of its natural qualities, but above all through its spiritual power, as oil blessed and transformed into the power of the Spirit (*epiclesis*). So in the *Canons of Hippolytus* it is said that for the sick to be able to have recourse to the church means 'a medicine ordered to their cure', since there they can receive the 'water of prayer' and the 'oil of benediction' (*eujelaion*).[16] Innocent I (c. 416) supposes that the oil blessed by a bishop can be used 'by all Christians, to carry out anointing with it in their personal needs or those of their family', thinking particularly of the need to heal the sick.[17] Cesarius of Arles in his *Sermons* (c. 503–4) draws special attention to this healing purpose of anointing, as opposed to the magical and superstitious practices of the pagans, to which Christians felt drawn, and against which he stresses the virtue and healing power of the anointing of the sick carried out by the church.[18] He addresses himself to mothers, who, if their children are sick, should try '*cum oleo benedicto a presbyteris (eos) perungere*'; to the sick who are capable of reaching a church, telling them: '*ad ecclesiam recurrite, oleo vos benedicto perungite, Eucharistiam Christi accipite*'; to Christians weak in faith, who should also have recourse to blessed oil, trusting in the words of the Apostle, '*secundum quod Jacobus Ap. dicit*'. 'Cesarius seeks to foster a general and spontaneous recourse to anointing in order to supplant the magic rites of healing handed down by paganism . . . He speaks of the sick in general, without making any allusion to whether their situation involves risk of death or not.'[19] Bishop Eloy of Noyon (588–660) expresses the same concern in recommending the faithful not to go to 'magicians, or soothsayers, or witches, or charlatans . . . ', but to use blessed oil 'to anoint their bodies with it in the name of Christ . . . and so recover health not only of body but also of soul'.[20] The Venerable Bede (672–735) likewise testifies to the custom handed down from the apostles that 'the sick should be anointed by priests with consecrated oil and be healed through the prayers that accompany this'.[21]

So while these authors are aware of other uses of oil, they relate it to the anointing of the sick and here give it a healing power and intention, always related to the blessing it has received from a minister of Christ and by virtue of the power of the Spirit. Nowhere do they distinguish between a less and a more serious disease, implying a difference of required minister and effect.[22] Nor do they make any distinction between 'anointing-sacrament' and 'sacramental anointing', in order to determine its effect and efficacy.[23] It is not clear whether the blessed oil they continually refer to is always the same oil applied or used in every case. What is clear, though, is that all physical or spiritual power attributed to the oil derives from its consecration and blessing.[24]

Anointing was not the only rite performed for the sick; the laying-on of hands was also regularly used, as Irenaeus indicates: 'Others cure those suffering from some sickness through the laying-on of hands, and send them back healthy.'[25] St Eutiquius (512–82) describes the cure effected on a young man when, 'using various prayers, he laid his hands on the boy, and anointed him with the blessed oil'.[26] St Ambrose (333–97), commenting on Mark 16.17ff., recalls that the laying-on of hands has curative power through the grace and power of God.[27] The *Ambrosian rite* itself includes the 'laying-on of hands on the sick person' as an integral part of the celebration of anointing, which indicates that it too had a healing function.[28] However, one should not lose sight of the fact that the rite associated with possible healing was, by definition, anointing with oil.

(c) In liturgical texts

The preceding section has shown that the Christian value of anointing resides in the blessing. This is also brought out by the liturgical texts, where the following elements indicate the importance attached to blessing: it is reserved exclusively to the bishop, or to the presbyter in his absence; it has been liturgically ordered from the earliest times; it is placed within the solemn setting of the Eucharist. The oldest of these formulas of blessing is

found in the *Apostolic Tradition* of Hippolytus, where it is applied to the
healing and blessing of the sick.[29] The *Apostolic Constitutions*,[30] the
Euchologion of Serapion[31] and the *Testamentum Domini*[32] also hand on
blessing formulas of varying length and detail. The oldest Roman
sacramentaries, the Gelasian[33] and Gregorian,[34] which are related to the
Apostolic Tradition, have other formulas. Of all these, the *'Emitte'* formula
is the one that became most widespread, owing to the richness of its
content and its literary structure. It was embodied in successive sacramentaries and liturgical books, and survived to our own day (though
reformed in the new Ritual).[35] The formulas found in the *Liturgia
hispanica* (seventh and eighth centuries)[36] are also significant for their
concrete references to the situation of sickness, their insistence in asking
for integral healing of body and soul, and the stress they place on the
primacy of the action of Christ and the Spirit.[37] The Eastern tradition is no
less rich in such formulas, found in its *'euchelaion'* rite[38] which clearly
evidences the complementarity between bodily curing and spiritual
healing or forgiveness of sins.[39] A comparative study of these formulas of
blessing points to the following conclusions:

Christian anointing differs from both Jewish anointing (Old Testament) and pagan anointing, not because of the ritual surrounding it, or
the form it takes, but rather on account of the consecratory blessing it
involves. Through this blessing the Spirit comes down on, takes
possession of, transforms, fructifies . . . the oil, in such a manner that
its application now implies a new strength and power of presence and
sanctification, of curing and integral healing, of full salvation and
forgiveness. The blessing gives the oil its true sacramental virtue, frees it
from magic, places it on the same level as the other sacramentals used by
the church, such as the blessed baptismal water.

Since the blessing was so important, it was reserved to the bishop (in
Rome and the dioceses most closely linked to it), but could be carried
out by the priest in the bishop's absence (in the East and Milan), and
during the first centuries was carried out during the solemn celebration
of the Eucharist.[40] From the tenth century, when the normal time for
blessing had been moved to Maundy Thursday, the distinction between
oil for anointing the sick and the oil of catechumens became blurred.
According to M. Ramos, 'the same receptacle could contain the oil to be
applied to one or the other, as we are told by Reginon of Prum (d.915):
"On Maundy Thursday every presbyter must bring two receptacles, one
for chrism and the other for the oil of catechumens and the sick".'[41]
Again according to Ramos, it is likely that originally no distinction was

made between 'the oil of the sick and the properly consecratory oil, to which the technical name of chrism was later reserved . . . The evolutionary process consisted of a progressive specialization in the blessing and usage of oils.'[42]

The actual application of the oil undoubtedly had a complementary and relative importance compared to the blessing. This meant that it could be carried out either by ordained ministers or by the faithful: '*non solum sacerdotibus, sed et omnibus uti christiani licet, in sua aut in suorum necessitate ungendum*' (Innocent I). The oil could either be applied or drunk: '*et sua sancta benedictio sit omni ungenti, gustanti, tangenti, tutamentum corporis, animae et spiritus*' (the '*Emitte*' formula). In view of the fact that its recipients could be both the slightly and the gravely ill, and bearing in mind the number of current illnesses and the limited numbers of ordained ministers, it was logical to extend this faculty to lay people, who were always close to their sick relatives.

The hoped-for effect of anointing, the texts show, was above all a physical healing or cure, to which the spiritual effect or forgiveness-salvation was normally added. The most common expressions are those that ask for a physical cure, and those that ask for the integral or total healing of the sick person: '*mens et corpus*', '*corpus et peccatum*', '*corpus et anima*', '*interius et exterius*', '*sanitas corporis et indulgentia peccatorum*' . . . This effect is never applied to specific illnesses only, but is asked for in all cases, as the Hispanic formulas in particular testify.[43] All this allows us to state that the early church understood the rite of anointing as a rite of physical healing, certainly, but above all as a rite of healing of the whole sick person.

3. Practices of healing

Having considered charisms and rites of healing, let us now take a quick look at the 'practices' in which these charisms were demonstrated and the rites embodied.

(a) In the New Testament

The New Testament shows an 'ordinary'[44] continuation of Christ's ministry, particularly in the practice of visiting and attending to the sick, widows and orphans, those truly in need (see James 1.27; Acts 6.1–2). James spells out this practice of visiting in his letter: 'If one of you is ill, he should send for the elders of the church . . .' (5.14). This is in fulfilment of Christ's own commandment: 'I was sick and you visited me' (Matt. 25.36, 45).

Besides this ministry, there is another 'practice' applied to oneself, implying both offering-up and ascesis in one's own sufferings, uniting oneself to the sufferings of Christ: 'Indeed, as the sufferings of Christ overflow to us, so, through Christ, does our consolation overflow. When we are made to suffer, it is for your consolation and salvation' (II Cor. 1.5–6). And elsewhere: 'It makes me happy to suffer for you, as I am suffering now, and in my own body to do what I can to make up all that has still to be undergone by Christ for the sake of his body, the church' (Col. 1.24).[45]

(b) In tradition

Early patristic witnesses also speak of the 'visit' as the most important practice in care and cure of the sick. A very brief survey: St Polycarp states that elders should 'take in the abandoned and visit all the sick, without forgetting widows and orphans'.[46] Hippolytus of Rome, referring to deacons, tells them that they should 'notify the bishop of those who are sick, so that he may visit them. For it is most comforting to the sick to know that the high priest is mindful of them.'[47] St Athanasius recalls that it is very sad for sick people not to be visited by anyone, since 'they consider this calamity more serious than their illness itself'.[48] And it is said of St Augustine that he followed the example of the apostle (James 1.27) in visiting orphans and widows in their sorrow, and in going to pray for the sick and lay his hands on them.[49]

Some texts also speak of a practice of exorcism in relation to sickness, as a counterpart to pagan magical and superstitious practices. St Cesarius of Arles is the most significant witness to this in the Western church; he attributes a certain exorcizing function to the very act of anointing, making it liberate from temptation and the power of the devil, from sicknesses and from sin.[50] In the Eastern church, John Mandakuni (405-87), for example, referring to those who employ superstitious means, reminds them of James 5.14–15, and adds: 'and those vexed by the malign spirit he ordered to throw him out by fasting and prayer, with the sign of the cross, which conquers all.'[51] The relationship established between anointing and prayer and fasting, in order to cure illness and expel devils, indicates that anointing, too, was seen as having a certain exorcizing character.

Liturgical texts produce no other practices than those related to the rite of anointing and other rites described above. It is worth recording here what the Nestorian Council of Mar Joseph (c. 559) laid down as liturgical pastoral practice: 'When one of those who have fallen into this sickness (superstition) is converted, let him be offered as a means of healing the same as those who are physically ill: the oil of prayer (*euchelaion*) blessed by the priests.'[52]

4. Conclusion

Given the diversity of churches, witnesses and liturgies, it would be foolhardy to attempt an overall generalization, but not to point out what is common and basic to all. There is a sufficient degree of concidence among the majority of sources to allow one to extract the doctrinal constants and most important practices.

(*a*) It seems clear that anointing with blessed oil, however generalized and widespread, cannot in any way be compared to the 'use of holy water'.[53] The importance, solemnity, dignity and 'sacramental' value of its blessing give it an extraordinary strength and power, and the people were conscious of this. Although the question had not yet been raised as to whether it was a sacrament in the strict sense, and it was not to be included among the seven, it was nevertheless recognized and valued in life as being a sacramental action. The sacraments existed as salvific-ecclesial realities of Christian life before becoming a concept and number defined in theological or conciliar formulations. To claim to determine the specific meaning of a sacrament by the meaning most commonly attributed to it in the scholastic period when the number was fixed at seven is to devalue permanent sacramental truth in favour of the temporal formulation or fixation of a sacrament.[54]

(*b*) There can be no doubt of the great importance attributed to the curative or bodily effect of anointing in the early centuries. In the light of the texts, one can neither undervalue this healing aspect of anointing by comparing it with other apotropaic or devotional means, such as holy water, nor reduce all its dimensions to this healing aspect, by comparing it with other magical or medical means. The physical cure spoken of is produced not by magic, but by grace, by the power of the Spirit and the response of faith. It is not a partial cure, but an integral one, for the health of body and soul, of the affected members and the sinful heart. This is perfectly understandable in a world that explained everything by the active presence of God, and understood prayer and signs as the true 'medicine of the poor'. In short, in the early church, neither the charisms, nor the rites nor the practices of healing, were reduced to the anointing of the sick. But it was in the anointing of the sick that these charisms, rites and practices were active, significant and concentrated with the greatest frequency and efficacy, with the greatest degree of recognition and solemnity.

Translated by Paul Burns

Notes

1. On the New Testament, see A. Oepke, '*Nosos*', *TDNT* 4, 1091–8; H. Greeven, *Krankheit und Heilung nach dem N.T.*, Stuttgart 1948; J. Hempel, 'Heilung als Symbol und Wirklichkeit im biblischen Schrifttum', *Nachrichten der Akad. der Wissenschaften in Göttingen*, I, Philos-hist. Kl. 3, 1958; G. Crespy, *La guérison par la foi*, Cahiers théologiques 30, Neuchâtel-Paris 1952; id., 'Maladie et guérison dans le Nouveau Testament', *Lumière et Vie* 86, 1968, 45–69; P. Fedrizzi, *L'unzione degli infermi e la sofferenza*, Padua 1972; B. Maggioni, 'Gesù e la Chiesa primitiva di fronte alla malatia', in *Il sacramento dei malati*, Turin 1975, 39–75; P. Mourlon-Beernaert, 'Jésus-Christ et la santé. Le témoignage évangélique', *Lumière et Vie* 3, 1985, 275–88; R. A. Lambourne, *Le Christ et la santé*, Paris 1972; F. Mussner, *Der Jacobusbrief*, Herders Theol. Kom. zum N.T., Freiburg 1967; J. Cantinat, *Les épîtres de S. Jacques et de S. Jude*, Sources Bibliques, Paris 1973; E. Cothenet, 'La guérison comme signe du royaume: l'onction des malades (Jc 5.13–16)', in *La maladie et la mort du chrétien dans la liturgie*, Rome 1975, 101–25; G. Marconi, 'La malattia come "punto di vista": esegesi di Gc 5.13–20', *Rivista Biblica* 1, 1990, 57–72.

On the Fathers and the liturgy, see: C. Ruch and L. Godefroy, 'Extrême-onction', in A. Vacant and E. Mangenot, *Dictionnaire de Théologie Catholique* V, Paris 1913, 1897–2022; F. Lovsky, *L'Eglise et les malades depuis le II siècle jusqu'au début du XX*, Thonon-les-Baines 1957; A. Chavasse, *Etude sur l'onction des infirmes dans l'Eglise latine du III au XI siècle. 1. Du III siècle à la reforme carolingienne*, Lyons 1942; M. Nicolau, *La unción de los enfermos. Estudio histórico-dogmático*, Madrid 1965; C. Ortemann, *Le sacrement des malades*, Lyons 1971; M. Ramos, 'Perspectiva histórica de la doctrina sobre la unción de los enformos', in *Los sacramentos de los enfermos*, Madrid 1974, 41–64; id., 'Notas para una historia litúrgica de la Unción de los enfermos,' *Phase* 161, 1987, 383–402.

2. Maggioni, 'Gesú e la Chiesa primitiva'(n.1), 39–41. This situation, with some minor changes, can be said to be common to both the time of Jesus and that of the early church (till the fifth century).

3. Cf. Lambourne, *Le Christ e la santé*(n.1), 73–105; F. Lage, 'Jésus ante la enfermedad', *Communio* 5, 1983, 405–16; Oepke, *TDNT* 4, 204: 'The most deep-seated image of Christ in early tradition is undoubtedly that of Jesus as prodigious healer.'

4. Cf. Cothenet, 'La guérison'(n.1), 107–8.

5. Cf B. Bagatti, *L'Eglise de la circoncision*, Jerusalem 1965, 212ff; Cothenet, 'La guérison'(n.1), 119–21.

6. Cf. Chavasse, *Etude sur l'onction*(n.1), 127ff.

7. Cf. J Lage, 'Jesús ante la enfermedad'(n.3), 415: 'We cannot precisely define the forces at work in faith-healing. But they are at work.'

8. Cf. H. Schlier, '*aleipho*', *TDNT* I, 229–32; P. Vallini, 'Le chrétien et l'huile sainte', *Christus* 42, 1964, 153ff; B. Reicke, 'L'onction des malades d'après Saint Jacques', *La Maison Dieu* 113, 1973, 50–6; Mgr Romaniuk, 'Unción en general y extrema-unción', *Communio* 5, 1983, 290–404; E. Cothenet, 'Onction', *DBS* VI, 701–32, in which he shows how the medicinal and even aesthetic/athletic use of oil offered an excellent basis for its use as a healing rite.

9. In effect, this relationship between the two rites has been brought out in the new Ritual. See the ICEL text Pastoral Care of the Sick: Anointing and Viaticum, 1982.

10. See the works cited by Mussner-Reicke, Cothenet, Cantinat, Romaniuk,

Marconi(n.1). See my synthesis in D. Borobio(ed.), *La celebración en la Iglesia II. Sacramentos*, Salamanca 1988, 691–4.
    11. *Adv. haereses*, I.1, c.214, 4, PG 7, 664.
    12. *In Lev. Hom.*, 2, 4, PG 12, 417.
    13. *Demonstratio*, 23, 3, Patrologia Syriaca 1, 2, 10.
    14. Achilis(ed.), *Constituciones Agipciacas*, 117; also in B. Botte(ed.), *Tradición Apostolica* 5, 18.
    15. *De Hier. Eccl.*, c.7.
    16, R. G. Coquin, *Les Canons d'Hippolyte*, Patrologia Orientalis XXXI 2, n. 6, (121) 389. Cf. 'Oración por los enfermos y unción sacramental', *La Iglesia en oración*, Barcelona 1987, 688 n. 27. Remember that the expression '*eujé-elaion*' is that used by the Byzantines to designate the whole rite: cf. J. Groar, *Euchologion sive Rituale Graecorum*, Venice ²1730 (I have used the facsimile reprint, Graz 1960), 332–46.
    17. *Carta a Decenio de Gubbio*, PL 20, 559–61; cf. Chavasse, *Etude sur l'onction*(n.1), 89–90.
    18. G. Morin, *S. Cesarii Arelatensis Sermones*, Maredsous 1937, vol. I, *Sermo* 13, 62–7; *Sermo* 50, 215–7; *Sermo* 52, 220–3; *Sermo* 184, 708–11. Cf. Chavasse, *L'onction*(n.1), 101–10.
    19. Ortemann, *Le sacrament*(n.1), 31.
    20. PL 87, 529 A-B.
    21. PL 93, 39–40; cf. Chavasse, *L'onction*(n.1), 123–4.
    22. This distinction is proposed, without sufficient basis, by P. de Letter, 'Anointing of the Sick', *Sacramentum Mundi*, Vol. 1, New York and London 1968, 37–40, here 38: 'There is further evidence, for the first five centuries, of a twofold anointing of the sick, a private one done with blessed oil by the sick person himself or his relatives, and a liturgical anointing performed by the priest or bishop . . . The first obviously supposes less grave illness and is meant for bodily cure (it pertains to the charism of healing). The second is for the case of grave illness and seeks spiritual help from the priest or bishop; it is the sacramental anointing.'
    23. This distinction is proposed by G. Greshake, basing himself on the very varied usage given to anointing in the early church: in grave or slight illnesses, to anoint a particular part of the body or the whole body, applying the oil as an ointment or taking it as a drink, as exorcistic practice (in dangerous places, with animals, in stables) or as magic medicine, 'Letzte Ölung-Krankensalbung-Tauferneuerung angesichts des Todes?', in *Leiturgia-Koinonía-Diakonía*, Freiburg 1980, 97–126, here 104–5; id., 'Letzte Ölung oder Kranken-salbung? Plädoyer für eine differenzierte sakramentale Theorie und Praxis', *Geist und Leben* 2, 1983, 119–36. I return to the subject later.
    24. Cf. Ramos, 'Notas para una historia'(n.1), 391.
    25. *Adv. Haereses* 2, 32.4, PG 7, 829B.
    26. 'Vida de San Eutiquio, narrada por Eustasio', *Acta Sanctorum Boll. 6 aprilis*, 558; Nicolau, *La unción(n.1), 40.*
    27. *De Poenitentia* 1.8, nn. 35–7, PL 16, 497ff.
    28. Cf. A. Triaca, 'Le rite de l'*impositio manum super infirmum* dans l'ancienne liturgie ambrosienne', in *La maladie et la mort*, 339–60, here 350, 356–7.
    29. *Tradición Apostólica*, ed.Botte, ch. 5, 18–19: '*Ut oleum hoc sanctificans das eis qui unguntur et percipiunt, in quo unxisti sacerdotes et prophetas, sic illos et omnes qui gustant conforta, et sanctifica eos qui percipiunt.*'

30. F. Funk (ed.), *Didascalia et Constitutiones Apostolorum*, Vol. 1, lib. VIII, ch. 29, 532.

31. Ibid., Vol. 2, *Testimonia et Scripturae propinquae*, chs. 17 and 19, 178–80, 190–2.

32. I. Rahmani (ed.), *Testamentum Domini nostri Iesu Christi*, Maguntiae 1899, lib. I, chs. 24–5, 48–9.

33. L. Mohlberg (ed.), *Liber sacramentorum Romanae Ecclesiae Anni Circuli*, Rome 1960, 61 n. 382; cf. A. Nocent, 'La maladie et la mort dans le sacramentaire gélasien', in *La maladie et la mort*(n.1), 243–60.

34. J. Deshusses (ed.), *Le sacramentaire Grégorien*, Fribourg 1971, 172–3.

35. The new Ritual proposes the reformed *'emitte'* formula as that for blessing the oil, on account of its epicletic content.

36. Well known formulas are: *in tuo nomine, Domine Iesu Christe, Omnipotens Deus* . . . See M. Ferotin, *Le liber Ordinum en usage dans l'Eglise wisigothique et mozarabe d'Espagne*, Paris 1904, cc. 7–11, 23; J. Janini, *Liber Ordinum sacerdotal*, Abbey of Silos 1981, 77–8.

37. Other significant formulas can be found in, e.g., the votive office *de infirmis*, as shown by J. Pinell, 'El oficio votivo "de infirmis" en el rito hispànico', in *La maladie et la mort*(n.1), 261–35.

38. J. Goar, Euchologion *sive Rituale Graecorum complectens ritus et ordines*, Venice 1730; H. Denzinger, *Ritus Orientalium, Coptorum, Syrorum et Armeniorum*, Viceburg 1863.

39. See the article by E. Melià, 'Le sacrement de l'onction des malades dans le développement historique et quelques considerations sur la pratique actuelle', in *La maladie et la mort*(n.1), 193–228.

40. The faithful used to bring the oil, together with other gifts, to be blessed during the Eucharist. At the end, each one collected his/her vessel and took it home for use. At least from the tenth century on, this blessing was transferred to Maundy Thursday. See M. Andrieu, *Les Ordines Romani du haut moyen-âge*, Louvain 1931ff.; on this point see *Ordo XXX*.

41. Ramos, 'Notas para la historia'(n.1), 391, referring to Réginon de Prüm, *De synodalibus causis* 1, 75, PL 132, 206.

42. Ibid. Although there is not sufficient textual evidence for a conclusive vindication of this opinion, it seems to me to bear all the marks of probability.

43. See the prayer *'In tuo nomine'*, tr. in Ortemann, Le sacrement(n.1), 23–4.

44. For a fuller treatment, see Borobio, 'Unción de enfermos',(n.1), 690–1.

45. Cf. Maggioni, 'Jesù e la Chiesa', 53–5.

46. *Ep. ad Philipenses*, VI, 1.

47. *Tradición Apostólica*, ch. 34, 81.

48. *Epist. ecycl.* 5, PG 25, 233.

49. Posidius, *Vita S. Augustini*, ch. 27, PL 32, 56.

50. *Vita Caesarii epic. arelat.* II, 17 (MGH Script. rer. mer. III, 451) says that when a possessed woman was brought:'*capiti eius manum imponens, benedictionem dedit, deinde oleum benedixit, ex quo eam nocturnis horis perungi iussit.*'

51. *Hom.* 26. Cf. M. Schmid, *Heilige Reden des Johannes Mandakuni*, 22ff., cited in Nicolau, *La unción*(n.1), 38–9.

52. Hefele-Leclerc, vol. III, app. 2, Paris 1910, 1204.

53. Greshake, 'Letzte Ölung-Krankensalbung-Tauferneuerung?'(n.23), 104–5.

54. Ibid., 105–8. I therefore disagree with the view he expresses.

The Anointing of the Sick in the Greek Orthodox Church

Basilius Groen

One finds the practice of anointing the sick in most Eastern churches. It has disappeared from the Armenian church since around the fourteenth century, and no longer occurs in the 'Nestorian' church; it is questionable whether it ever existed in the latter. In this article I shall not discuss the practice in all the Eastern churches, but limit myself to the practice in the Byzantine Orthodox Church, and within that to the Greek tradition.

Structure and name

Generally speaking, during the first millennium the anointing of the sick in the Greek Byzantine church consisted of only one or more prayers and smearing with oil. Sometimes the sick drank the oil. In particular from the third, fourth and fifth centuries we have a number of priestly prayers, the theme of which is anointing with oil. Important sources of this are the *Apostolic Tradition*, the *Canons* of Hippolytus, the *Apostolic Constitutions*, the *Testament of Our Lord Jesus Christ* and the *Euchologion* of Serapion of Thmuis. The liturgical and clerical emphasis lay on the blessing of the oil, not on the anointing. It was customary for laity to anoint themselves or others with the oil. During the eleventh, twelfth and thirteenth centuries, however, the rite spread relatively quickly. An important reason for this was that because of the plural in James 5.14 ('elders') and the practice in other churches, especially the Latin church, it was found that more than one priest had to be involved. The number of priests was defined as seven.

Each had his own part in the ceremony. The result of this development was a rite which may probably be regarded as the most complicated and longest in the Byzantine euchologion of the time (the liturgical book with the texts of the sacraments, the hours and important prayers). Despite later reductions, the anointing of the sick remained a mammoth rite. The formulary which is used today consists of four parts:

(a) *The introduction*. This consists of Ps. 143; Ps.51; the canon (a series of songs which was originally based on nine biblical canticles) and many kinds of other troparia (verses of songs). Here we have a kind of abbreviated mattins/lauds, a survival from the time when the anointing of the sick was preceded by a special morning service.

(b) *The anointing with oil*. After the litany of peace the prayer of consecration is spoken by the leading priest: 'Lord, who in thy compassion and mercy healest the wounds of our soul and body, sanctify this oil that for those who are anointed with it, it may serve to heal and do away with all passion, bodily sickness, defilement of flesh and spirit and all evil . . . ' After that more troparia are sung.

(c) The cycles of the seven priests. Each cycle is made up of an epistle, a gospel (both preceded each time by verses from the psalms), intercessions, two prayers and the anointing of the sick. Each time the cycle is led by a different priest. The first of the two prayers varies. The second, the prayer of anointing, is always the same: 'Holy Father, physician of the soul and body, you sent your only begotten Son, our Lord Jesus Christ, who heals all sickness and brings deliverance from death, heal also your servant (NN) from the weakness of body and soul that has him in its grasp, and make him live through the grace of your anointed [Christ] . . .' In the structure of this part it is easy to recognize that of the liturgy of the word from the Byzantine eucharist. The parallel comes from the time when the anointing of the sick and the eucharist were still connected.

(d) The absolution and dismissal. The last part consists primarily of a solemn prayer that was read when the evangeliar was placed on the head of the sick person, some troparia, and the dismissal.

The mercy of God runs like a scarlet thread all through the rite. In sometimes flowery and picturesque language it is shown how God is concerned for the fallen and sick and raises them up again. They and the priestly mediators also pray constantly that God will send down his healing power and heal the body and soul of the sufferers, that he will bless and sanctify them, forgive their sins and restore them to health.

The anointing of the sick is one of the seven sacraments (or mysteries) of the Greek church. The name most used for the rite is 'prayer of oil' (*euchelaio*). This term refers to the key elements of the celebration: prayer and oil. Another name sometimes used is the 'celebration of the seven popes' (*eftapapdo*). A third name, but one which is found only in books, is 'holy oil' (*agio elaio*). Both the first and the third names echo another word: 'mercy' (*eleos*). In the texts of the celebration one comes upon all kinds of word-plays on oil (*elaio*, pronounced *eleo*), mercy (*eleos*) and gracious (*ileos*).

Present-day practice

After this short introduction to the theoretical structure of the rite, let us now look at how the sacrament functions in practice at present. Here are seven linked cases. They are all set in contemporary Greece.

1. It is 19 November, the eve of the feast of St Andrew, the first of the apostles to be called. In the church of the Holy Apostles at Thessaloniki this evening there is a solemn celebration of the great vespers and the anointing of the sick, and the next morning, morning service and the eucharist; finally, at noon, there is the service of intercession to the saint. This evening it is raining cats and dogs, but the church is full to bursting. Most of the churchgoers are women, and only a small number of young people are there. After vespers, the anointing of the sick is celebrated from seven until half past eight. Seven priests stand in front of the iconostasis. Along with the choir they perform the service. Different parts are omitted, like the canon and long sections of the prayers, which are often very extended. Otherwise the service would go on too long. The people listen, holding lighted candles in their hands, and make the sign of the cross when they hear the names of saints and familiar passages from the Gospels. Sometimes they join in the singing, when the choir sings a well known troparion. Before the celebration began, people had written their names and those of members of their family on pieces of paper, and at the same time had put money in the offertory box intended for the poor or for priests. The names are read out by the popes either softly or aloud during the service and brought 'before God's presence'. After the dismissal there is a prayer about the meaning of the sacrament. Only after that does the anointing take place. Each person is anointed. However, no one looks sick. During the anointing the priests say 'for the healing of soul and body' or 'oil of gladness in the name of the Father, the Son and the Holy Spirit', or something similar. The parts of the body which are anointed (in the form of a cross) are often the forehead, the cheeks, the chin, the palm of the hand and the back of the hand. After it is over, a number of people take oil home with them. There they anoint members of the family who were not present in church, or they keep the oil for use in case of sickness.

Here are a few general comments before we look at the next cases. In each parish church, cathedral or monastery church the anointing of the sick is celebrated at least once a year, on the Wednesday or Thursday of Holy Week. In addition, it can take place during the period of fasting which precedes Christmas and which can run from 15 November to the festival itself. On Mount Athos the anointing of the sick is celebrated two days before Christmas. In all these instances the anointing of the sick functions as a means of preparation for the great feasts of Easter and Christmas, above all for the receiving of communion during these festivals. Some people also go to confession; for others the anointing of the sick replaces confession. There are also some priests who first anoint believers with consecrated oil 'for the healing of soul and body' each time they administer communion. The anointing of the sick also serves 'for the wellbeing' (*gia to kalo*) of all participants, from the village or the city. 'It can only do you good, never make you worse,' is the view of many laypeople. By contrast, the priests stress the function of forgiveness, physical and mental healing, and sanctification, that the anointing of the sick conveys.

Furthermore, the anointing of the sick in the church of the Holy Apostles in Thessaloniki takes place after the dismissal. Why? The fear is that there would be chaos in the full church if the people had to come forward to be anointed during the service. Of course people are not anointed by each priest but only by one. On Athos all priests anoint all monks; normally a monk is anointed there fifty-six times during a celebration.

2. It is the period of the great forty-day fast. In the afternoon pope Pavlos, who is in Galatista, a village in Macedonia, goes to a family which has asked him to come and celebrate the anointing of the sick. That is a good custom and a respected tradition in many places. The whole family is present; so too are other more distant members of the family, neighbours and a number of friends. On the table is an icon, a dish of flour with seven candles in it, and a glass of olive oil with a burning wick and some wadding. All the people hold burning candles in their hands. The priest puts on his stole. The rite begins. The priest omits the canon, numerous troparia and a great many prayers. The rest of the people listen attentively, but at the same time the children are playing with one another. The scene is both informal and pious. Beforehand the women have cleaned and polished the house, as part of the Lenten preparations; the children are washed, and people have put their best clothes on. Now only the soul has to be washed by the anointing of the sick. Each person is anointed. No one in the house is physically sick. When the rite is over the pope may sit down. He and the other guests are offered coffee, orange juice and sweetmeats. The flour is later baked into bread by a woman who has had no sexual intercourse with a man. The bread is used in the eucharist.

Here essentially we have the same kind of anointing of the sick as in the previous case. This kind also takes place above all during the great forty-day fast, Holy Week and the Christmas fast, and sometimes also during the 'fasts of Mary' in the first two weeks of August. The differences between it and the first case are of course the different surroundings (a home instead of a church) and the involvement of only one priest. However, this one priest performs a rite which is meant for seven popes. It is also striking that here, too, large parts of the formulary are omitted. That is a general custom, but there is no uniformity here. One pope omits one part, another a different one. At the moment the celebration of the anointing of the sick in Greece is in chaos. It can also happen that a priest performs the whole rite, but so that it does not go on too long (an hour and a half to two hours) he rushes through the texts and as a result it is difficult to understand him,

3. The Jannopoulos family in Patra has recently been burdened with serious problems. Mother does not feel well, her own mother has recently died, and there is a threat that her husband will be made redundant. She fears for the future and resolves to ask the pastor to her home to come and celebrate the anointing of the sick.

In this case the celebration takes place to prevent things getting worse, so that they may get better, and so that physical, spiritual and material prosperity may not be destroyed. Again it is 'for wellbeing'. It is also quite customary for a parish priest to be asked to come and perform an anointing of the sick in the new home when a family moves. Our rite here banishes evil and ensures happiness. People are not yet used to the new house. The unknown provokes anxiety. The anointing of the sick has to guarantee a good start as a rite of transition.

4. Jannis Kalogas in Thessaloniki has cancer. His wife and children know it. The pastor knows it. Everyone knows it but him. Nobody has wanted to tell him. The pastor comes to visit him and suggests that he performs the anointing of the sick. The family strongly support the suggestion. 'It will do you good,' Jannis is told. 'Make your confession and receive communion.' However, from the way in which his wife and children talk to him and from his own worsening condition Jannis understands what people mean and do not dare to tell him in so many words. He agrees to the celebration of the anointing of the sick. After the service he makes his confession and receives communion. The next day his health gets dramatically worse. He is immediately taken into hospital and dies three days later. On the day of his death the pastor again wants to perform the anointing of the sick, because 'after the first time the patient felt very close to God and the rite helped him in his preparations for death'. But death itself is quicker and thwarts the priest's plans. In this case the

anointing of the sick shows striking parallels with Roman Catholic extreme unction and with the *ritus continuus* in which the anointing of the sick, penitence and the last rites are celebrated or administered one after the other.

5. Sofia Dimitrakou, a young woman of twenty-five who lives in Thessaloniki, keeps feeling very depressed. So she has stopped work and is undergoing psychotherapy. Her parents are very worried about her. Her mother first asks the pastor to celebrate a special eucharist to heal her daughter, but she later changes her mind and asks for the anointing of the sick at home. Both Sofia and her parents take part in the ceremony. After it is over the priest wishes Sofia a speedy recovery. He has known her a long time and also knows about her problems, though only superficially.

6. Petros Chalvadis, who lives in Sparta, goes to confession. His penance is to have an anointing of the sick at home. Here our rite serves to fulfil his penance.

7. In the Red Cross hospital in Athens the chaplain, Father Dimitrious, always has oil with him when he visits patients on the wards. If during a pastoral visit a patient wishes it, the pastor gets out the oil, says the prayer of anointing, 'Holy Father', and anoints the sick person. This ritual takes only a couple of minutes.

The anointing of the sick is celebrated above all at the end of the great forty-day fast, during the first three days of Holy Week, and during the pre-Christmas fast. It is performed as a preparation for the coming festival and 'for wellbeing'. The types mentioned in cases 1, 2 and 3 are the most frequent. In a minority of cases the anointing of the sick is performed for the physically sick and for terminal patients. The reasons for this are that people find that this rite serves as a preparation for Easter and Christmas, or that the anointing of the sick is regarded as a prelude to death and so they prefer to keep it away; or people have dissociated themselves from the church and its sacraments, are indifferent to them, and prefer to trust just the doctors. The original context, the *locus proprius* of the anointing of the sick, is, however, sickness (physical sickness). So the instances practised most often and the theory of the 'seventh sacrament' do not correspond. Many Greek theologians or priests therefore feel compelled to argue that the practice and the aim of the anointing of the sick do in fact correspond. They point to the close connection made in the Bible between sin and sickness, and stress that all people are sinful and thus sick. They argue that no one is one hundred per cent healthy, and that each person can carry around a hidden ailment in his or her body. Therefore they feel that an anointing of the sick is always appropriate. Prevention, they say, is better than cure.

Other rites

There are many more rites than the anointing of the sick for restoring health, driving out evil or avoiding it, or 'for wellbeing' generally. The most important of these are the blessing of water, intercession to Mary or a particular saint, the 'rite for the consolation of sick people who are tormented by unclean and aggressive spirits', prayers for the sick and exorcisms, confession, sick communion, a private eucharist with a special intention (not to be confused with the Western private mass), processions and pilgrimages, above all to the ikon of Mary on the island of Tinos in the Aegean, to the relics of Saint Spyridon on the island of Corfu, and so on. In addition there is special anointing in monasteries 'for the healing of soul and body' at the time of the festival of the patron saint of the church. At home, in case of sickness or other problems, people sometimes take a bit of oil from the lamp which burns before the house icon and anoint the sick person or themselves with it. Finally, there is 'liberation from the evil eye': the woman of the house takes olive oil and water and with it three times makes a cross on the forehead of the person who does not feel well (usually a sudden ailment), says a silent prayer or 'Our Father', and also sometimes spits three times in the face of the anointed person, to undo the influence of the 'evil eye'.

To end with, here are some reflections on the practice of the anointing of the sick.

The pastorate

The anointing of the sick is only the tip of an iceberg. Below the surface of the water is the great mass of pastoral care, the content of the liturgy. The question has to be raised: what happens in the church in addition to liturgy? Is the church really there for its members, especially its sick members? Does it also support them outside worship? Does it stand alongside them? Challenge them? Or are rites simply performed without further pastoral care? In the last instance the so-called tip of the iceberg is not a top at all but a mini-iceberg which soon melts. In the Greek Orthodox Church, in practice one usually finds two views and attitudes. The more prevalent is that the main task of the church is to perform the sacraments. Only the liturgy leads to union with God and brings God's kingdom into the world. Pastoral care is valuable, but only serves to lead people to the sacraments. If it does not do that, it is useless. It is important to understand that liturgical catechesis plays an important role in this way of thinking.

The other 'school' is convinced that this attitude in fact often leads to ritualism. This school stresses that good pastoral care is indispensable. The questions it asks are illustrated in the following example. If a girl of nineteen goes to a priest and asks for anointing of the sick because she cannot find a good husband, and if the priest then celebrates the rite at her home, is given money for it, wishes the girl success and goes away again, what good is that? Does the woman now meet her lifetime partner? If the priest does not try to discover why the woman is so upset because she is not married, if he does not give her an opportunity to talk about her problems and does not listen to her and help her to cope better with the difficulties of her life, why then celebrate the anointing of the sick? In that case it becomes something magical. The anointing of the sick functions well only within the context of proper pastoral care, namely as a dramatization – the Greek theologians concerned understand the word *drama* as action, liturgical action – as a symbolizing of the making whole of human beings, their salvation, body and soul, by God. Although it is growing, the second school is still very much smaller than the first.

The language

The language used in the anointing of the sick is Byzantine Greek, while the psalms and reading represent an even earlier phase of Greek, the Septuagint translation and the Greek of the New Testament. Above all, the epistles and the troparia pose a problem, because they have quite a complicated style. Most Greeks nowadays understand only part of the texts. The degree to which they do so depends on their upbringing. Most Greeks have not had any further education. Above all in the villages there are even a great many priests who scarcely understand the texts because they have only been to lower school. Moreover, in general, knowledge of ancient Greek is steadily diminishing. Although most lay people and not a few priests are in favour of translating the church rites into modern Greek, many other popes and almost all Greek bishops feel that the liturgy must remain as it is. In their view the inspired text of the Septuagint, the original text of the New Testament and the sacred songs and prayers are treasures of the Orthodox tradition which must not be touched.

A related problem is that of the active participation of the people in the ceremony. As long as people do not understand the rite and its texts, it is difficult to urge them to participate more actively.

The stipends

If a priest presides at an anointing of the sick at home, he is usually paid for it. The amount varies between one and ten US dollars (say, between 50p and £5). This custom dates from the time when the income of the priest depended on the stipends that he received for celebrating the sacraments. However, nowadays the popes get a salary from the Greek state. Some priests are no longer willing to accept money from the faithful, saying that they do not need a double income and that they want to avoid the criticism that the clergy are moneygrubbers. There are even popes who because of the question of stipends never suggest the celebration of an anointing of the sick to faithful that they do not know well. However, most priests accept the money that they get. They say that one cannot refuse a gift, and that stipends are a good tradition. A lot of young people and left-wing circles feel bitter about this. They get the impression that the priests are first of all thinking about their own pockets.

Crisis of identity

At the moment, great changes are taking place in Greece and other countries where the Greek Orthodox church has been established for a long time. Urbanization, emigration, the influence of Western industry, Western 'civilization', its ethical values and mass tourism, the increased extent of higher education and the development of modern medical and nursing health care have brought about radical changes to many traditional values. So there is an identity crisis. Numerous people are asking who they are, what being Greek means, what Orthodox is and what the Greek Orthodox Church stands for. Those who structure the church (bishops, priests, theologians, monks and nuns) generally argue that the spirit of modern times is one of technocracy, rationalism, luxury, materialism, tension and uncertainty, and that there is only one way out of the crisis, namely life in accordance with the tradition of the Orthodox church. In this tradition the liturgy has a central place. It is also said that people need to hallow themselves by repenting and doing good works. The three spiritual stages of purification, transfiguration and divinization are often cited as a model. In the doctrine of faith and in canon law the first seven ecumenical councils play a major role. The study of the church fathers is also thought to be indispensable. The most popular fathers are John Chrysostom, Basil, John of Damascus and Gregory Palamas. The Byzantine empire is glorified as an utterly Christian society, as God's Orthodox kingdom on earth. Most church leaders think that the tradition is unchangeable. The present-day church needs to keep its faith and hand it on intact.

However, it is a fact that most Greek Orthodox do not feel, or no longer feel, that the language of their spiritual leaders speaks to them. The church plays a constantly diminishing role in their lives. The old 'sacral' society in which church and state, civil and canon law, were closely connected, in which the liturgy was public worship, *cultus publicus*, is rapidly falling apart. Moreover because of secularization many people no longer experience the combination, the being thrown together (*symbolo*) of God's grace, human happiness and material things like bread, wine, oil, salt and water in sacramental celebrations. The consequence of that is that the anointing of the sick is celebrated increasingly rarely, and is less and less being seen as a means of becoming whole and of coming into contact with the holy.

Translated by John Bowden

Bibliography

J. Dauvillier, 'Extrême-Onction dans les Églises Orientales', *Dictionnaire de Droit Canonique* 5, 1953, 725–89
I. Fontoulès, *Akolouthia tou Euchelaiou*, Keimena Leitourgikès 15, Thessaloniki 1978
B. Groen, *'Ter genezing van ziel en lichaam'. De viering van het oliesel in de Grieks-Orthodoxe kerk*, Nijmegen 1990.
E. Mélia, 'Le sacrement d l'Onction des malades dans son développement historique et quelques considérations sur la pratique actuelle', in *La maladie et la mort du chrétien dans la liturgie*, Rome 1975, 193–228.
Mikron Euchologion è Agiasmatarion, Athens [8]1981
T. Spáčil, *Doctrina theologiae Orientis separati de Sacra Infirmorum Unctione*, Orientalia Christiana 24.2, Rome 1931.
E. Suttner, 'Die Krankensalbung (das "Öl des Gebets") in den altorientalischen Kirchen', *Ephemerides Liturgicae* 8, 1975, 371–96.

Healing in Africa

Meinrad Hebga

The wording of the title might give rise to some misunderstanding. Clearly in so restricted a space there can be no question of covering such a vast and complex subject as that of healing in Africa. So I shall limit myself to a few aspects of the question which seem to me to be essential. I shall outline them briefly in this introduction.

The nature of treatment in Africa
To understand healing in Africa it is necessary to consider it in its own framework, in its socio-cultural context, and not through the distorting lenses of foreign anthropologies or cultures, set up as a universal norm of reference. So I shall recall successively the pluralistic scheme of the 'human composite' which underlies the technique of traditional treatments, our conception of sickness and healing, the forces involved in sickness and treatment, and finally the essential characteristics of African therapy.

African treatment and Christianity
In this second part we shall investigate the relevance of the Christianization of African therapeutic rites and the inculturation of the official rituals received from the Western churches. It goes without saying that it is through the description of our everyday practice that elements of a value judgment will appear, and that it will be possible to express some wishes and – why not? – make some suggestions.

I. The nature of treatment in Africa

The success of certain works which more or less amount to folk lore, describing the action of those who are called 'African healers', is largely due to the fact that our traditional treatment is irrational, because it resorts to more or less bizarre beliefs and practices, spirits, rites for removing spells, evocative gestures, mysterious formulae, garish accoutrements, and a panoply (of instruments and medicines) which is 'so close to nature'. Now as well as being a legitimate sense of scientific and technological superiority, this condescending judgment is a function of a dualistic anthropology (which others would say was diffusionist and unifocal), according to which humanity is divided into two subgroups, of which one, the West, is the unique centre of universal civilization and is called to spread over the other. Or it has to be observed that there is no justification for arguing from the universality of science to strictly metaphysical conceptions. Metaphysics is in no way the sphere of objective and scientific knowledge, but the sphere of conjecture and imagination. Consequently, the dualistic scheme of the 'human composite' (body-soul), which is that of the Western philosophical and anthropological tradition, is not a criterion for Asian or African pluralistic schemes, nor should the monistic scheme of ancient Hebrew thought be considered irrational.[1] To understand our traditional method of treatment, therefore, it is necessary to relate it to our conception of human beings, the subjects of sickness, treatment and healing.

1. The 'human composite'
    In African anthropology, the scheme of the 'human composite' is at least triadic, comprising the body, the breath and the shadow. Certain cultural regions add a term which is translated 'spirit'; yet others mention the heart, the name. Body, breath, shadow, heart, and so on are in no way the elements, the components of an entity. We might call them instances of the person, levels of being of which each one is the entire person from a particular point of view. The body is not a thing, but the manifestation, the epiphany, of a person during his or her earthly life and in the beyond. The breath is the same person alive, and the shadow the human being considered from the aspect of agility – others would say of immateriality.

2. Our invisible partners
    The Africans feel that they have a relationship not only with the living, their kin, but also with the spirits, ancestors or dead who do not enter into this noble category; the same is also true of the different types of genies: *vodun, kinkirsi, miegu, mamiwata*, etc. All these personal beings are potential partners in the process that leads to sickness, or procures healing.
    Doubtless it is necessary here to justify our beliefs in genies and spirits. I do not think that the objections raised in the name of science to biblical or New Testament angelology are of particular interest. If the existence of

God and spirits cannot be scientifically established, it would also be vain to pretend that we could provide a scientific proof that they do not exist. The religious or mystical approach to phenomena is quite legitimate in its own sphere, and verbal explanations borrowed from the vocabulary of psychopathology like psychoneurosis, hallucination, demonopathy and so on no longer impress. To carry conviction it would be necessary to establish the presence of a particular psychological pathology in a determinate case and not sweepingly to reject embarrassing facts, resorting to portmanteau formulae. Most of all, vocabulary with a scientific colouring is unacceptable.[2]

3. The African conception of life, sickness and death

It is interesting to note that in a number of Bantu languages the term denoting life is identical to that which denotes survival, perseverance in the prerogatives of the so-called living being. This suggests a concept of life as a force struggling against the forces of destruction which threaten us on all sides, which use us, sometimes in an underhand way (time, age, chronic illness) and sometimes brutally (a wound, an acute crisis). It is perhaps this idea that Fr Tempels wanted to suggest by his famous theory of the being-force which in his view characterizes Bantu ontology.[3] The vital force can grow or decrease, and when it is weak, sickness ensues, following an indefinite gradation. Some stages of this process of decline are serious enough for Africans simply to call them 'death'. These include fainting and what European medicine calls coma, or clinical death, not to mention the last journey to the limit, to crossing the point of no return which by our way of speaking is definitive, or total, death. Our scale of death is truly a matter of degree: one can be slightly dead, very dead, or completely dead.

Another African approach to sickness is to consider it as a lack of balance between the patient and his or her physical or social entourage, between the patient and other living (and indeed dead) beings. For example, the sterility of a woman may be attributed to the malice of a mother-in-law or the wrath of an ancestor. Restoration of balance will be achieved by a treatment comprising sacrifice and reconciliation. It would be wrong to do away with this approach too quickly, on the pretext that it is based on causalities which have not been established. For example, the anxiety caused by relationships of conflict with someone whom we value excessively may do considerable damage to natural mechanisms like breathing or the circulation of the blood, and ultimately cause a serious ailment that can lead to death. Thus if, rightly or wrongly, the sick person is subsequently persuaded that the ancestor or mother-in-law is now appeased, the psychological relaxation that he or she feels can prompt a return to normal, i.e. to the health that could not have been obtained solely by physical medication.

4. Forces at work in sickness and healing

First it is necessary to dispel the misunderstanding that to African eyes no sickness or death are natural. We know very well that people die of wounds, poisoning, burning, drowning; that the bite of a venomous snake or a ferocious beast can be fatal. But even in cases of this kind we still sometimes speak of enchantment, to indicate that it is not by chance that such and such a misfortune happened to me rather than you, that I found myself in range of a viper or a leopard, or that a tree fell at the very moment when my brother was passing underneath. A malevolent will must have arranged the circumstances at someone's expense. Is the mentality of those who attribute fortunate or unfortunate happenings to providence, beyond physical causality, so remote from that of Africans? The only difference is that providence is thought to be good and benevolent, whereas I presuppose that enchantment manifests an evident will to harm. Let us now look at the forces involved in sickness and treatment.

The power of things

It is beyond question that the good traditional doctors know dozens of medicinal plants and barks, and are masters in using them to heal or to harm, although their knowledge is not scientific but empirical, and they are criticized for often giving only an approximate dose. Advisedly, to close up wounds, they resort to the Indian pine (*Jatropha curcas*, of the family of the euphorbia). Its kernels are rich in fixed oil and curcines. The leaves and fruits provide alkaloids, and its latex tannins.[4] Against intestinal parasites, the Beti of the Cameroun use the 'nkanela' (*Pseudopondias microcarpa*, of the anacardic family), or papaya seeds. Sometimes a beneficial or maleficent effect is attributed to horns decorated with particular substances or special stones, for example the *mpuma* stone of the Basaa in the Cameroun. But human bones win the prize for occult power: the initiated absolutely refuse to reveal the nature of this power to profane people like us. Straddling a human bone, even without knowing it, can cause a dangerous, even mortal, ailment. Sometimes, by contrast, a bone will be applied to a sick person as a reputedly effective cure.[5]

The power of language

Among all peoples a certain power is attributed to language, that is, to a significant word or gesture: as we read in Genesis, 'Let there be light: and there was light.' However, in this respect the human being, too, is a kind of

God: blessings or curses are thought to produce the effects mentioned. Besides, in traditional treatments, the virtue of the plants or barks or other kinds of medicine is reinforced and orientated by the formula which wards off evil and begins the process of healing. This power of the word is in fact that of the healer, and Africans consider it to be both innate and acquired: at birth it is only a potentiality which will guide and reinforce initiation and apprenticeship. We might ask whether this is not something similar to what is expressed in other cultures by the image of the gift of healing recognized in certain people, a gift which would remain at an embryonic stage were it not later brought out by apprenticeship and practice.

5. Essential characteristics of African treatment
Traditional treatment has characteristic features which I shall now try to bring out.

Integralist medicine
This expression is perhaps inadequate to translate the idea that the object of this medicine is the sick person as a whole – body, breath, shadow, spirit, heart – and not sometimes the organism and sometimes the psyche of which Western dualism speaks. The concept of the psycho-somatic, which is relatively recent in scientific medical theory, is related to this approach. In other words, for us Africans it is absurd to claim to care sometimes for one's physical part and sometimes for one's mental part; it is the person a whole who is ill, although the morbid ailment only manifests itself in a particular part of that person.

Community medicine
As we have seen, sickness is the sign and expression of tensions, conflicts, breaks in equilibrium in the relationship of the individual with others. In a sense it is not just the individual but also the social group which is sick and must be restored by treatment. Hence the holding of discussions and the sacrifices for reconciliation among the living, or between them and the dead, sacrifices which often include a meal of fraternal communion.

Liturgical medicine
This is a real celebration, with the involvement of spectators, or at least some actors, visible or invisible. The drama is played out between the officiant and the forces of good on the one hand, and the sickness and the forces of evil on the other. This liturgical aspect of African treatment explains the possible recourse to singing, dancing, dialogue between the officiant and the audience, or even with invisible beings. We shall see how

these characteristic features of traditional treatment could be and should be taken up by the Christian liturgy for the sick in black Africa.

II. African treatment and Christianity

The general attitude of Christian missionaries to African treatment of sickness was and remains negative: a mixture of disdain for 'all this primitive hotchpotch', and horror at 'pagan superstitions'. Those who approached it in a spirit of calm and objective study were rare. Even rarer were those who showed open sympathy.[6] On the whole African clergy, both Catholic and Protestant, adapted without further ado the approach of their foreign masters. Without going to the trouble of patient research and discernment by trial and error, many of them resorted to summary condemnation, if not repression. Their hostility towards traditional treatment often extended to the diaconia of the sick exercised by clergy and laity within our churches. And as, rightly or wrongly, this diaconia is associated with the movement for charismatic renewal, this movement has become the *bête noire* of numerous priests, pastors and bishops, despite the favourable attitude to it in their churches or among the higher authorities. In their eyes, some syncretistic deviations justify the baby being thrown out with the bath water.

Nowadays this policy of facility and flight forward is less and less convincing. Syncretistic healers have rebelled against the canonical sanctions hurled at them, taking with them in their revolt numerous followers who are more sensitive to spiritual healing than to theological and disciplinary discourse. It is no longer possible to dodge the work of discernment and adaptation that is necessary. And the question has to be asked: do the traditional African rites have to be Christianized, or is it enough to inculturate the official rites handed on by the Western churches?

1. The Christianization of therapeutic African rites

It is imperative to integrate some of our major therapeutic rites into the Christian panoply being used among us. In fact the specific needs which gave birth to them are still there in our society, and we do not have the impression that they are effectively met by the contribution of the sacraments and sacramentals, rich though this may be.[7] The reason for this feeling of dissatisfaction with the spiritual means put at our disposal by the church is that they do not mention our ills by name or the forces that act upon us. The cultural framework of their application is alien to us.

So we must begin from the needs of the people to whom we are sent, from their experiences, and not from general views borrowed from distant nations. It is not enough to say that sorcery and spells do not exist in an attempt to reassure people, or to send them to hospital to solve all the problems from which they suffer and die. Besides, all too often scientific medicine gives up and repeats *ad nauseam*: 'Negative, nothing to report.' Which amounts to saying to a comedian, 'So my patient died from an excess of health!' It would not even be enough to recite a gospel or a ritual prayer over the sick, or to invoke the powerful name of Christ over them. In addition, it is necessary to name explicitly in a loud and intelligible voice the formidable forces of the *famla*, the *kon* or the *nson* to ward them off.[8] The faithful who have been put on guard against the *tsoo* or *likan li bihut* rites to which the Beti and Basaa of the Cameroun resort to purify themselves from incest, or to guard against the consequences of certain flows of human blood, are only appeased and reassured if, in our prayer of deliverance, we protect them against every eventuality within the framework of the ancestral tradition. That is the strategy adopted by priests, pastors and laity, with encouraging results.

But these experiments by pioneers will have only a very limited scope as long as they are not officially taken over by our churches. So on the Catholic side it is necessary to take account of the completely new attitude of openness shown by the Sacred Congregation for Divine Worship in its *De Benedictionibus*, promulgated on 31 May 1984. There we read: 'It is for episcopal conferences to examine with care and prudence that which it could be good to accept from the traditions and genius of each people, and thus to suggest other adaptations that might be thought useful or necessary.'[9]

In other words, the authorities responsible for Catholic worship in Rome recognize the inconveniences of a universal ritual, of which the absence of contextualization is not the least. So they are inviting the churches whose particular cultural features have never been taken into account to adapt the Roman rites for their own people. As far as we are concerned, that amounts to constructing African rituals, which are then to be submitted for the approval of Rome. That is good news, and no time should be lost in creating *ad hoc* commissions, according to national or regional groups. I suppose that our Protestant brothers and sisters are, by tradition, more free in their movement in this sphere than we are.

It must also be noted that the African adaptation of a rite which is Western in conception and realization, is inculturation and not the Christianization of indigenous rites. Now it is this last operation which is the unequivocal sign of an authentic cultural pluralism in the Christian churches. Here are a couple of examples. I find myself confronted with a typical case of 'staining of consanguinity', in this case a case of incest. I try to adapt the traditional *basaa* rite, since for reasons of Christian morality I cannot apply it as it is. This rite, the *likan li bihut* mentioned above, should take place in public, preferably at a crossroads, in the presence of the families of the offenders and the leading figures of the village. The officiant offers as sacrifice a ram and a sheep, and pairs of birds, lizards, centipedes and insects. Those involved in the incest are asked to repeat their criminal act before the audience so that it will be for ever impressed on their consciences. Then the entrails of the sacrificed animals, mixed with different barks and herbs, are applied still burning to the bodies of those concerned by the officiant, who pronounces several times the ritual formula, 'Ban on the genitals, ban on the vulva.' The audience, the utensils and the places are sprinkled with the blood of the victims.

I work in the utmost secrecy. I invite the offenders to take account of the gravity of their fault and to repent of it before God and before their families or their representatives. Then I read a penitential psalm, and kinsfolk are sprinkled with holy water and then anointed with holy oil blessed for this purpose. Thenceforward purified and taken in charge by the Lord, they no longer have to fear the consequences that popular belief attaches to incest; physical and social decline, a curse on posterity, and so on. To my knowledge persons thus reconciled with God and with family society do not feel the need to resort to the traditional rite or to any maraboutage. Just to say that there was no causal link between the crime and physical or social decline would not dissipate the anxiety of those haunted by atavistic fears.

It seems to me that a discernment which is as communal as possible helps to detach those parts of the ancestral rite that a Christian could not retain, namely the sacrifices, even addressed to the God of Jesus Christ, since for us from henceforth the one perfect sacrifice is that of Christ; the evocation of the spirits which are thought to come and possess the sick, or to exercise vengeance on the supposed aggressors of these last; the repetition of the incestuous act; and the publicity given to the rite of expiation and reconciliation, except where this is necessary to remedy a public scandal. On the other hand, one could keep, even if it meant explaining it in an appropriate catechesis, the symbolism of the pairs of animal sacrifices and the expression of family or clan solidarity both among the living and between them and the dead, in the sin and its expiation, a solidarity which justifies the communal celebration of a penitential rite.

2. The inculturation of Western rites

Given the centralism of the Catholic church and the existence of a universal ritual for the whole of the Roman communion, Africans should never dream of obtaining the right to create entirely original rituals. Besides, that is not desirable, since a common core contributes towards strengthening unity in the faith, and allows the members of local churches to feel at home everywhere. It would already be interesting if in addition to the Christianization of some of their traditional rites, Africans were allowed to adapt prayers, objects and gestures borrowed from other civilizations to their own needs. Here too we are once again in a period of lone pioneers. But there is room for hope that commissions officially nominated by the competent authorities will bring together experiences from all over the continent and be in a position to suggest structures and coherent projects for the approval of the bishops.

In villages supposed to be dangerous because of sorcerers and other soothsayers, I proceed in the following way. I collect independent evidence of the situation, and receive individually some sick people who are considered to be under a spell or even possessed. Resorting to psychopathological texts, I make a summary diagnosis of each of them. They are often people who have already been treated by various practitioners of traditional medicine, who have been to hospitals and to the Jamot Centre for neuropsychiatry, or whose medical examination has ended with a desperate 'nothing to report'. It is then time to restore them to their own social and cultural context. In fact the symptoms are a language, and as such they are at least in part dependent on a particular sphere of life, collective representations, and atavism. And the treatment which takes these different factors into account has resources which are lacking to hospital medicine. On the other hand I have complete faith in the name of Jesus Christ by which we are healed (Acts. 4.10), of Jesus from whom a healing power emanated (Luke 6.19) and still does so. So I am not surprised when an illness which resists pharmaceutical therapy or neuropsychiatry or a paralysis which has defied the ultramodern techniques of the Centre de Garches in France, along with the efforts of a number of traditional doctors, can sometimes yield, God willing, to an African Christian rite. Here, as an example, are some extracts from my little ritual for particular occasions.

Prayer of deliverance for an 'infested' village

Antiphon: Arise, Lord, come to our aid! Deliver us for your name's sake! (Ps. 44.27)
Prayer: Lord, you are the Father of all, you do not want the death of sinners but that they may convert and return to life. So we do not ask you to destroy our enemies, the sorcerers and sorceresses bent on doing evil, but to prevent them from doing harm. Inspired by Satan and by other evil spirits, they sow sickness and death; by poison and evil they destroy

the health of the people, the fields, trade, and the understanding and peace of families. Others infest houses, dwellings and entire villages. Lord, convert these servants of evil and death, and pardon them. But if they refuse and are bent on destroying your children, may their own evil deeds return against them, so that he who kills by the sword himself perishes by the sword (Matt. 26.52) . . .

Lord, destroy the reign of Satan in this village. Tear it from the darkness of fetishes and sorcery and introduce it into Christ's kingdom of light . . .

Since the sorcerers are shedding innocent blood, God will give them blood to drink (Rev. 16.16).

And the people shall say Amen.

This kind of intervention delights the faithful and causes real panic among the malefactors. Sometimes these latter discretely leave the chapel where they have come to scoff at their victims, and sometimes the event shows that they were not wrong to flee.

3. The example of the independent churches

While the Catholic church in Africa is still taking its first tottering steps towards a non-sacramental diaconia of the sick, numerous dissident or independent churches have long experience in this area from which we can benefit. Knowing their society well, the founders of these communities have primarily sought to emulate, even to exceed, the prestige of their opponents, the sorcerers, magicians and traditional therapists. This concern to dethrone the spiritual leaders of the clan, village or whole region, to reign in their place in the name of the gospel, appears clearly in the iconoclastic zeal of those who burst out in fury against sorcery: William Harris on the Ivory Coast, Alice Mulenga Lenshina in Zambia, Gaudencia Aoko in Kenya, Simon Kimbangu in the Belgian Congo, which is now Zaire. For the traditional rites they substitute others that could be called syncretistic, but not in a pejorative sense. So in the Congolese movement called Croix-Koma, founded by Victor Malanda in 1957, new members make a solemn renunciation of sorcery and debauchery, declaring:

I will no longer have friendship with Satan, Croix-Koma!
I will no longer have friendship with Satan and the fetishes, Croix-Koma!
I renounce resorting often to women (or men), Croix-Koma![10]

Confraternities like Croix-Koma practise healing by prayer and the laying on of hands. Some seem to have kept ancient usages like purification with lustral water, the public confession of sins, and a meal of brotherly communion.

The example given by the independent churches clearly has to be subjected to a Christian and African evaluation, as do the experiences of Catholic pioneers: these are not compulsory models.

Conclusion

There could be no question of treating all aspects of such a vast and complex subject in so limited a space. I would like simply to conclude by stressing the duty of contextualization which falls on those concerned with the diaconia of the sick, contextualization at two levels: that of the Christianization of several local rites and that of the inculturation of rites which have come from the West. This is long-term work which it is all the more urgent to begin. The obstacles are well known. Some people stress the diversity of local traditions and think that there is only one solution to the problem, the imposition of the universal Western ritual. Others, above all among the church authorities, think that Christianity cannot salvage what more or less immediately has a smell of paganism. Furthermore, commissions have been set up in the past which in the end have achieved nothing apart from elementary working methods. It is for our churches to understand what is at stake in a ministry of the sick which is truly Christian and authentically African. They need not only to take it up fully but also to promote it with determination, in both the pastoral and the financial spheres. This positive action will prevent too frequent recourse (which is of doubtful effectiveness) to the repression of real or supposed deviations, of which pioneers become guilty when left to themselves. The harvest is plenteous, but the workers are few and impoverished.

Translated by John Bowden

Notes

1. Claude Tresmontant, *Essai sur la Pensée Hébraique*, Paris 1962, 89–117; Balbir Singh, *The Conceptual Framework of Indian Philosophy*, New Delhi 1976, ch.5: 'Atman'; Meinrad Hebga, *Rationalité d'un Discours Africain sur les Phénomènes Paranormaux et Conception pluraliste du Composé Humain*, PhD thesis, Sorbonne, Paris (typescript), Vol.1, 101–66.

2. 'Neurosis': a disease of the personality characterized by unresolved psychological conflicts which inhibit social conduct; 'psychoneurosis': a neurosis in which the psychological conflict is very elaborate; 'demonopathy': the delusion of someone who feels possessed by a demon.

3. According to Tempels, for Western thought force is the attribute of being, while for the Bantu all being is a force.

4. M. Hebga, *Sorcellerie. Chimère dangereuse?*, Abidjan 1979, 257. Alkaloids are organic substances some of which have therapeutic properties, for example morphine. Tannins are substances contained in vegetables and are preservatives for skins.

5. Does not the Roman liturgical rule which seeks for mass to be celebrated only on an altar containing the relics of a martyr, an altar which the priest kisses before turning to the people, relate to such a mentality?

6. I mention among others, E.de Rosny, *Healers in the Night*, Maryknoll 1985; Masamba ma Mpolo, *La Libération des Envoûtés*, Yaoundé 1978.

7. A sacrament is a sacred ritual act instituted by Jesus Christ and intended for the sanctification of the faithful; a sacramental is a sacred rite instituted by the church.

8. *famla, kon*, is sorcery thought to cause the apparent death of the victims, used to the enrichment of their master.

9. *Rituel Romain*, Chalet-Tardy 1988, 13.

10. Sinda Martial, *Le Messianisme Congolais*, Paris 1972, 336ff.

How Malagasays Face Illness

Adolphe Razafintsalama

As a teacher and seeker, I am not well placed to write about the pastoral practice of anointing the sick: such a practice happens to me only occasionally. So the reflections that follow will be more theoretical.

In talking of this sacrament, many of my colleagues who are writing for this issue of *Concilium* will have noted two things: first, the profound development prompted by Vatican II and given specific direction by the *Ordo Unctionis Infirmorum* of 7 December 1972; secondly, in the dynamic of this evolution, the possibility of adapting the rites in conformity with the character of each culture.[1] In other words, the Roman *Ordo Unctionis* can still be the object of further development.

Now it has to be said that in this sphere the episcopal conference of Madagascar has not yet had time to study the problem: so far it has been able only to translate and comment on the text of the Roman *Ordo*.[2]

It is to justify the need for further development of the rites of the anointing of the sick that I would like to lay here the anthropological foundation on which the church might reflect on this sacrament in a new way.

To do this I shall proceed in three stages:

How Malagasy people face sickness and old age;
Care of the sick and the old;
The anointing of the sick: future perspectives.

1. How Malagasy people face sickness and old age

If the aim of the anointing of the sick is the healing of the soul and possibly of the body, it is logical that one should first investigate the conception that a particular culture has of soul and body. Now it has to be noted that the contribution of anthropology and Western theology to Madagascar has blurred the traditional conception, but has not destroyed it completely.

(a) The Malagasy conception of the human being

The theology of Western origin which nurtures our theologies and our catecheses (both from the Catholic side and from the Protestant or Anglican side) has in practice confirmed the Thomistic conception of human beings with its Aristotelian background, namely their hylomorphic composition, the fact that they are made up of a body and a soul. At death the 'matter' dissolves, and the soul of the righteous goes to heaven: body and soul have to await their reunion at the final resurrection.

Malagasy Christians have assimilated this conception, but only partly. In fact traditional rites and prayers reveal that the archaic anthropological conception remains largely alive. Schematically, it can be summed up like this. According to an old myth, the Earth Mother, spouse of the Heavenly Creator, fashioned the first man and the first woman of clay; but it was the Heavenly Creator (*Zanahary*) who breathed life into these inert statues. The breath of life (*fofon aina*) also goes back to *Zanahary* at death, while the Earth Mother repossesses the body.[3] There is no specific idea of what happens to the breath of life.

However, the dead person does not become nothing. In fact, in addition to the breath of life and the body, the human being possesses a double (*ambiróa*). As long as someone is in good health, no one is generally preoccupied with his or her existence, with the exception of sorcerers who could cast an evil spell through the visible shadow (*áloka*) which is the symbolic projection of the invisible double. However, the community begins to become disturbed when for no apparent reason someone loses appetite, becomes noticeably thin and totters when walking; could it be that the *ambiróa* is beginning to leave for the realm of the dead? Among certain tribes, when that happens, recourse is had to rites to recall the *ambiróa*.[4]

Such rites seem to have become quite rare. But what is more general – even among many Christians – is a preoccupation with the future of the double after death. In fact, of the various aims of funeral rites, two relate to this future: the first is concerned with the removal of the double from the sphere of the living, for such a double is supremely dangerous; it has to be removed respectfully but firmly, otherwise it will be transformed into a fatal *ambiróa* or *ángatra*, which will torment the living, sometimes to the point of drawing them into the kingdom of death. The second objective of the rites is to transform this same double into a protective ancestor (*rázana*): these are rites of passage which one could describe as apotheosis and which attain their climax in the strange celebrations of second funerals or *famadíhana*, which generally take place a year after the first.[5]

(b) The Malagasy conception of sickness

If that is the Malagasy conception of human beings, that of sickness will necessarily be influenced by it. Like all other cultures, Malagasy culture knows that certain illnesses are brought on by 'natural' causes: a variety of accidents, lack of prudence (misconduct, drink and so on), parasites, etc. Modern access to scientific knowledge clearly increases the sphere of such knowledge. And in the same way, Malagasys use both traditional medications, based on the knowledge of the properties of 'simples', and modern medications.

But as will have become evident in the previous section, Malagasys do not have just a unilaterally materialistic or rationalistic view of human beings; they also have a magical-religious view. That is why sicknesses with a natural cause and, even more, others which take strange forms, have dimensions that are either transcendent or magical and are linked either to divine justice, to the immanent justice called *Tódy*, or to the wrath of the ancestors. But worst of all these causes, because they are the most difficult to master, are the *mosávy* or sorceries, an expression of all kinds of social tensions. Furthermore, certain tribes know kinds of trance which are attributed to the possession of a person (usually a woman) by a royal ancestor: this is the famous *trómba*.[6] The Protestant churches readily assimilate these trances to demon possession and consequently practise exorcism.

(c) The Malagasy conception of old age

A mature age, and old age in particular, is considered by Malagasays to be a normal human achievement. As long as the old man is in possession of his faculties, he is the obligatory counsellor of the extended family or clan; such people open family or clan meetings, even if their children have been to university or achieved a higher status, and even if, in the end, the advice of these latter must count in the final decisions.

But once old people lapse, as they say, into infancy, there is no question of putting them in a hospice – except in case of extreme necessity (and in any case hospices are rare). Filial love means that the grown up children in turn lavish on them the care they received in childhood, '*mitáiza*', i.e. cradling, bringing up with tenderness. This is *válim-ba-béna* (literally carrying children – here old people – on one's back) or, in the dialect of the Betsileo tribe, *mampiántitsa* (secure [happy] old age).

In certain tribes these old people are called *ràza*, living ancestors. Moreover their death is only a sweet passage to the state of *ràzana*, protectors in the other world; it is said that these old people are already on the way of return, *làlan 'ny mòdy*. Now, if their funerals are celebrated with some reservation by the Christians of the High Lands, elsewhere they are celebrated with jubilation and dancing, as in the case of the rites of second funerals or *famadíhana* which have already been mentioned.

The Malagasy ideas about human beings, sickness and old age described above are certainly evolving, as does any social and religious reality. However, because they are so basic for Malagasy culture, these ideas are evolving slowly. The same goes for the way in which the Malagasays rally round the sick: that is what we shall be considering in the next section.

2. Care of the sick

I have just been talking about the care taken over the old; that must be sufficient treatment of the subject. I would note simply that because of the generally positive attitude to old age, old people often accept their approaching end with stoicism. Custom decrees that they make their wills in time, and some even go so far as to make arrangements for their future funerals.

The attention given to the sick is more complex. But one can symbolize its quality by the well known saying *'ny maràry andríana*, 'the sick person is a prince'.

One can distinguish different forms of attention, following more or less ritualized sequences:

(a) Information (filazàna)

When a member of a nuclear family is fairly seriously ill, the event is no longer confined to this small circle: the members of the extended family (at least the descendants of the same grandparents) and the in-laws of the sick person (if he or she is married) have to be told quickly. So too have close friends, the village, members of associations or professional groups. Depending on the case, certain members of the parish can be involved, including the priest. All more or less serious illness is a more or less imminent threat to the integrity of the different groups concerned, in particular if death is on the horizon.

(b) Visits and offerings

The persons or groups who have been told must visit the sick person as soon as possible, either at home or in hospital. When they reach the sick person, the visitors have to express their stupefaction at such unexpected news, then ask how the illness came about and how the patient is faring. If the sick person is not too tired, he or she has to begin to describe the different phases of the illness. Otherwise members of the close family have to tell the story. The visitors then offer comfort, possibly suggesting some medical remedies. The visit always ends with an offering in kind (a chicken to make hot soup, sweetmeats) or money.

When the visitors have gone, one or more members of the close or more extended family have to watch over the sick person, even in a hospital where the presence of nurses makes this unnecessary. Moreover, the family will bring the sick person not only delicacies, but also dishes cooked at home; hospital food is – or is supposed to be – insipid . . . It is a tough task, but always conscientiously performed by the family.

As for medical care, the maximum is done, in accord with the expression *miàla nénina*, and to prevent in advance any cause for regret at not having done enough to look after the sick person. Hence the recourse to all kinds of medications, prayers or conjurations, traditional or modern. In a really serious situation the family will make vows to the ancestors and to God that a bull will be sacrificed in the event of a cure, or (if the family is Christian) there will be vows to some saint or the Trinity . . . Then, if the sick person should die, the grief of the family – though profound – will be mitigated; death will then be attributed either to destiny (*làhatra*) or to God or – if the family is truly Christian – to the Father.

If, on the other hand, the sick person has not been able to receive the correct care, as in the case of a tragic accident, failings in hospitalization and so on, the disquiet and grief of the family will be immense. That is one of the reasons why families – above all peasant families or poor families – only send their sick to the hospitals at a very late stage, either because the hospitals are badly maintained, because of bad reception by the staff, or simply because the administration is somewhat anonymous.

3. The anointing of the sick: future perspectives

As a better foundation for the new perspectives, aimed at a more inculturated development of theology and the pastoral work of the sacrament of the sick, we have had first to touch on the significance of Malagasy ideas about the human person, sickness and old age. The constraints imposed on this article mean that I can do no more than stress four major aspects of this conception which have already been brought out:

The human person is a composite being made up of body, breath of life, and a double;

Human beings, and indeed sickness and old age, have a dimension
which is both natural and transcendent (magico-religious);
The medications used have the same dimensions;
There is a strong presence of the family and social community around
the sick and finally the deceased person.

Whatever the ambiguity of these aspects, the anointing of the sick cannot
fail to take account of them, if it is not to risk forming a more or less
artificial addition to the ancient beliefs and rites. We have hardly begun on
renewals in this direction. Moreover, what I suggest here can only be a
direction for theological and pastoral research. Without claiming to be
exhaustive, I shall make four suggestions.

(a) Acceptance of traditional Malagasy anthropology
For reasons which would take too long to explain here, the first
missionaries – both Protestant and Catholic – rejected tripartite Malagasy
anthropology relating to the human being (body – breath of life – double)
and preferred the Thomistic perspective with a hylomorphic base (body/
soul). Moreover, to do this missionaries used another Malagasy concept
(which in fact is of great value), *fanàhy*, as a forced translation of the
Thomistic concept of soul; but *fanàhy* in ordinary literary usage denotes
wisdom. So there is an imbalance between traditional anthropology and
Christian anthropology. This would be a hair-splitting dispute if the
Malagasys had assimilated the new anthropology perfectly, but in the
majority of cases they have not. As I have pointed out, at crucial moments
of life their old concepts resurface, like their old beliefs: the patient who
grows thin for no obvious reason feels his double leaving him; on the death
of a beloved, the living, though Christians, are at the same time
preoccupied with the *fanàhy* or soul which goes to heaven and the double
which has to be integrated urgently into the sphere of guardian ancestors,
and so on. It is the same with ideas about sickness and the medications to be
used.
At this stage an indispensable preliminary to developing the anointing of
the sick in Madagascar will be to transform the ancient ideas in the light of
the gospel; unless this happens, the churches in Madagascar will still suffer
syncretism of beliefs and practices for a long time.

(b) Efforts that are already possible
While waiting for such deep inculturation to come about, we can already
start on certain renewals either in catechesis, or in visits to the sick, in order
to meet certain basic requirements. Here are the main ones:

We can show how anxiety over serious illness makes sense in Jesus Christ, who himself was ready to be subjected to such anguish (Matt. 26.38), but ultimately found peace because of his immense trust in his Father (cf. also Heb. 5.7–10);

We can show how the various malevolent forces (those of destiny, of the impassible God, the angry ancestors, jealous sorcerers and so on) have been defeated by the Risen Christ (Col.1.15–22) . . .

However, contrary to the Protestant churches, which describe certain of these forces – the *trómba*– as demons, I would not recommend exorcisms: without discernment, abuse of this rite can only increase the anxiety.

But since sorcery is most often the expression of family and social tensions, visiting the sick can be the occasion for suggesting meditation on the forgiveness of offences which Christ showed right up to the cross.

The most difficult task is to evangelize attitudes about the future of the 'double' after death. Such a concept is basically a symbol of anxiety about a premature death in the prime of life: the indication of this is that the end of an old person 'full of days' (*vóky ándro*) provokes virtually no anxiety. The book of Wisdom tried to resolve this scandal in its own way (ch.4), but the life of Christ, who died at the height of his powers, is a living response to such anguish.

Finally, the destiny of the guardian ancestor is a challenge to the sole mediation of the glorious Christ. On this point I have myself tried to develop a new theological approach would could form the basis for simpler catechesis and more effective pastoral work.[7]

(c) The presence of the family and social community
On this point, as we have seen, the tradition of attention to the sick is solid. The most difficult thing, in the event, is to provide a better integration of the carers and the other employees of the hospital, and to renew the institution of the hospital itself, so as to give it more of a 'family' face.

From a pastoral point of view it is also necessary to make more tangible the presence of the church, the body of Christ, in visits, in such a way as to go deeper than the purely sociological and psychological level. In other words, there is a need to establish a stronger link between visits and the gestures of Christ and the apostles and the expectation of the kingdom (Luke 7.21–22).

(d) The ministers of the anointing of the sick
For the present-day Western church the minister of anointing is

necessarily the bishop or priest. That is possible for countries and regions provided with priests and almoners who are available and near. But as P. Rouillard has commented, such a requirement becomes purely utopian for many regions of Latin America or the mission countries.[8] I can think of a priest in a coastal region of Madagascar who until a year ago had only his legs with which to cover a territory of more than sixty square miles; but even in the High Lands, where people are better situated, Fr de Brousse goes to celebrate the Sunday eucharist only two or three times a year in each of his twenty or thirty churches and chapels. In these circumstances it is usually the catechists or members of the parochial committee or members of a pious association who can represent the church to the sick or who can go to funerals. Only people living in cities can possibly receive unction (and then only if the priest is not travelling or on leave).

In these conditions could not the church diversify its practices, according to the usage of the earliest times?[9] That could be done in two ways:

In the absence of priests, qualified lay people would have the power to administer anointing;

Again, in a spirit closer to ancient practices, just the blessing of the oil could be restricted to the bishop or priest; but the use of it (in anointing, and why not in tasting?)[10] could be left either to the patient or to the members of the believing community close to the sick person.

Conclusion

As a conclusion: in line with the perspectives that I have just sketched out, it is certainly possible to develop the anointing of the sick in a new direction which integrates faith and culture. The task remains of persuading the episcopal conference of their pastoral community. Once this approach had been made, Rome would surely understand – in the dynamic of the Council – that in mission countries and in many other regions there would be a risk that the anointing of the sick remained a luxury sacrament reserved for city dwellers with priests, and not a sacrament for the poor – unless they were encouraged to bring about a profound transformation.

Translated by John Bowden

Notes

1. Vatican II, *Constitution on the Sacred Liturgy*, nos.38, 63, 75.
2. Navone, *Ny Sakramentan'ny Fanosoranany marary* (The sacrament of the anointing of the sick), Ambozontany 1983.
3. Faublee, *Récits Bara*, Paris 1947, 345–7.
4. H. Dubois, *Monographie des Betsileo*, Paris 1938, 734–8.
5. A. Razaitsalama, *Ny Finoana sy ny Fombany* (Beliefs and rites, duplicated text in Malagasy), Tananarive 1978, ch.10, the 'Razana' (the ancestors).
6. J.-M.Estrade, *Un culte de possession à Madagascar: Le Trómba*, Anthropos 1977.
7. A. Razafintsalama, 'Quand l'homme malgache dit Ancestre', *Telema*, January–March 1988, 11–29.
8. P. Rouillard, 'Le Ministre du Sacrement de l'onction des Malades', *Nouvelle revue théologique* 101, 1979, 395–402.
9. See the historical sections in B. Sesbouë, *L'Onction des Malades*, Fourvières 1971; C. Ortemann, *Le Sacrament des Malades*, Lyons 1971; A. G. Martimort, *L'Eglise en prière*, Tournai 1984, Vol.III, 'Les Sacraments'.
10. Hippolytus of Rome, *Apostolic Tradition*.

III · Critical Questions

Religion, Health and Illness

Meredith B. McGuire

Several socio-historical processes have resulted in a situation in which the linkage between religion, on the one hand, and health, illness and healing, on the other hand, has become sufficiently problematic as to warrant such attention as this journal issue. We shall briefly examine some of these processes (specifically, institutional differentiation of religion and medicine, the medicalization of many aspects of life, and the rationalization of medicine). Each of these processes has produced significant problems for sick persons, as well as social structural impediments for both religion and medicine in dealing with the needs of the sick. Finally, this article raises some challenges for new (rather than refurbished old) responses of religion to the distress and suffering of the ill and dying.

Sources of Disjunction

What processes have made the relevance of religion to health and illness problematic? Why should our society doubt that religion is an integral part of promoting health, healing illness, and responding to the needs of the suffering and dying?

Institutional differentiation

Whereas traditionally illness and healing were interwoven with numerous other institutional domains (especially religion and the family) Western medicine has gradually become differentiated from these other institutional spheres. Long before there was any distinctive occupation of medicine, healing was the function of mothers and other nurses, herbalists, folk healers, religious persons, midwives, and so on. The differentiation of medicine involved the development of a distinctive body of knowledge, a corps of specialists with control over this body of knowledge and its application, and public acknowledgment (or legitimacy) of the authority of medical specialists. While this differentiation has its roots at least as far back as early Greek and Persian medicine, only in this century has medicine become sufficiently legitimate and specialized to achieve professional dominance, carving out a large domain of functions previously shared or controlled by religion, the family, and other institutions (Freidson 1970).

Furthermore, institutional differentiation has wrought extensive internal specialization in modern Western medicine, due in large part to the growth of large-scale, bureaucratic settings for the learning and practice of medicine and to powerful underlying assumptions in the paradigm of biomedicine itself (discussed further below). One byproduct of the institutional differentiation of modern medicine is that it focuses on diseases – identified as discrete pathologies – rather than on sick persons. If we accept that such specialized attention to biophysical pathologies is sufficient for healing, then there is no reason to ask what religion has to offer the sick. This differentiated model of medicine relegates religious responses to illness to peripheral (albeit valuable) non-healing roles, such as comforting the dying or helping persons with chronic illnesses or disabilities to cope with their conditions. This medical model both limits the effectiveness of medical curing (as discussed further below) and underestimates the potential of non-medical sources of healing.

Medicalization

The notion of health is a *social ideal* that varies widely from one historical period to another and from one culture to another. Nineteenth-century America, for example, defined the ideal upper-class woman as pale, frail and delicate; robust health implied a lack of refinement. In other periods, cultures or subcultures, however, 'health' might be identified with traits such as physical prowess, fertility, spirituality, fatness, or youthfulness. Each culture's values regarding well-being and desired human qualities are embodied in its ideal of health.

Sickness is thus a form of deviance (i.e. a departure from group-established norms). According to Durkheim, the very existence of social norms – however defined – means that there will be deviance in all societies. He argued that societal reaction against deviance 'is above all designed to act upon upright [nondeviant] people . . . ' ([1893] 1964: 108). Thus, the response to sickness serves to reaffirm, for the sick and the well alike, a culture's norms and ideals.

One central function of social responses to sickness is social control (i.e., society tries to contain its members' behaviour within its norms by means of deterrents, incentives, rewards and punishments). Whether the social group punishes the individual depends largely upon its determination of whether the individual is responsible for the deviant behaviour. For example, people's response to the sick varies according to judgment of whether sick persons are malingering, or perhaps brought the sickness on themselves, or are 'innocent' victims of a malady. Throughout history, religious, legal and medical institutions have been important agents of social control in three main respects: definition of deviance, determination of responsibility, and administration of punishment.

Most modern societies have experienced a *medicalization of deviance*; that is, medical definitions of deviance and methods of social control have prevailed, eclipsing religious and other approaches to deviance. In effect, badness has become sickness (Conrad and Schneider, 1980). The appeal of medical definitions of deviance as 'sickness' is understandable. Religious definitions appear too nonrational and, in religiously pluralistic societies, lack society-wide acceptances. While they seem more rational, legal definitions of deviance appear to depend too much on human decisions, such as the judgment of a jury of ordinary citizens. By contrast, medical definitions of deviance appear to be 'scientific' and rational, based on technical expertise rather than human judgment.

Sickness, as the medicalized concept of deviance, is *not* a neutral scientific concept, however; it is ultimately a moral concept, establishing an evaluation of normality or desirability (Freidson 1970: 208). The apparent rationality of medical diagnosis masks an essentially evaluative process. The medical profession has continually expanded the definition of deviance to include as 'sickness' a wide range of disapproved behaviour: alcoholism, homosexuality, promiscuity, drug addiction, arson, suicide, over-active child behaviour, child abuse, and civil disobedience (see Conrad and Schneider 1980). Furthermore, the professional dominance of medicine in most Western societies has resulted in the medicalization of many 'normal' processes of life: fertility, pregnancy and childbirth, child feeding and training, menopause, aging and dying have all come under the aegis of medical advice and control (Zola 1983).

This process of medicalization has effectively reduced the legitimacy of alternative definitions of health and illness (such as those proffered by religious groups). It has simultaneously reduced the power of sick persons, families and non-medical authorities to make decisions about important areas of life, health, sickness and death.

A central feature of the institution of medicine in modern Western societies is that the function of curing disease has been radically separated from the function of providing meaning and a sense of belonging to the sick person. The medical institution has limited itself to the cure of *disease* (a biophysical entity) and the physical tending of the diseased person. Physicians do not typically address the person's *illness*: what the sickness means to the person, how it is experienced, how it affects the person's life, emotions, and personal relationships (Kleinman 1988). The meaning- and belonging-providing functions of healing are treated as relatively unimportant and are relegated to the private-sphere institutions of religion and family. Modern medicine generally views issues of meaning as unrelated to the cause or healing of health problems. Thus institutional structures are separated – both as domains of authority and as social-physical space.

To decry this imbalance of authority wrought by medical dominance is not, however, to suggest a return to the kind of exercise of authority over these areas of life that was historically exerted by religious groups. Nevertheless, medical authority is neither morally neutral nor capable of providing real guidance if solely based upon technical expertise. For example, using only technical criteria, medicine cannot speak definitively to many of the difficult moral decisions surrounding suffering and dying (see, for example, the ethical and policy issues raised in Callahan 1987, 1989). While retaining safeguards of tolerance and freedom of choice, modern societies need to develop institutional structures which give legitimacy and social space to groups which provide their members with guidance, social-emotional support, along with concrete care in the face of their troubles (see Levin and Idler 1981). While such groups would include traditional sources, such as traditional religious and family groups, they might also include non-medical healers (such as *espiritistas*), non-traditional religion (such as psychic circles), non-traditional forms of family (such as non-married partners), and non-traditional support groups (such as those in which persons suffering the same illness or crisis experience provide mutual help).

Rationalization of medicine

Another aspect of modernization that influences the relationship of religion to health and healing is *rationalization*, the application of criteria of functional rationality to many aspects of social and economic life. Applied to the division of labour, rationalization promotes bureaucratic forms of organization and an emphasis upon efficiency, standardization and instrumental criteria for decision-making, as exemplified by the

modern hospital. Rationalization also emphasizes rational ways of knowing, like the use of empirical evidence for explaining natural phenomena
without reference to non-natural categories of thought. A byproduct of this
rationalization is a focus upon technology and technique for transforming
rational knowledge into rational mastery.

Modern Western medical knowledge is built upon several assumptions
about the body, disease and ways of knowing. These assumptions are
products of a long history in Western thought, but they have created mixed
results for health and healing. The medical model assumes a *mind-body
dualism*, in which physical diseases and their causes are presumed to be
located strictly within the body (Engel 1977; see also Gordon 1988;
Kirmayer 1988). According to the medical model, the body can be
understood and treated separately from the person inhabiting it (Hahn and
Kleinman 1983).

While the philosophical foundations for this mind-body dichotomy
may go back to Descartes' separation of *res cogitans* and *res extensa*, the
practical foundations probably were laid in the late eighteenth- and early
nineteenth-century shift to medicine's emphasis upon clinical observation
and pathological anatomy. Foucault (1973) demonstrated that medicine
shifted its ways of viewing the body, developing a 'clinical gaze'. Whereas
previously physicians 'saw' the body indirectly (such as through patients'
own descriptions of their illness experiences), the clinical gaze empha-
sized direct clinical observation and physical examination. Increasingly
sophisticated pathological anatomy resulted in diseases conceptualized in
terms of alterations in tissues visible upon opening the body, such as in
surgery or autopsy. This approach to conceptualizing disease had a
profound effect of separating body from all aspects of mind (e.g.,
thinking, feelings, spirit) in the practice of clinical medicine (Sullivan
1986: 344–5).

A second assumption of modern medicine is *physical reductionism*,
holding that illness can be reduced to disordered bodily (e.g., biochemical
or neurophysiological) functions. This physical reductionism, by
definition, excludes social, psychological, spiritual, and behavioural
dimensions of illness (Engel 1977). The result of this reductionism,
together with medicine's mind-body dualism, is that disease is localized in
the *individual* body. Using such conceptions, modern medicine is poorly
equipped to deal with distress in the *social* body or with the impact of the
individual's social or emotional life upon physical health. Another result of
such narrow localization of disease is medicine's general inattention to
social conditions that contribute to illness or could aid in healing. For
example, a video display terminal operator who develops carpal tunnel

syndrome and an ulcer is probably suffering from work-related physical and emotional stress, but the reductionistic focus of medicine views these problems as located in the individual's body rather than the unhealthy conditions of the person's employment.

A third assumption of the Western medical model is what Dubos (1959) called the *'doctrine of specific aetiology'* – the belief that each disease is discrete, caused by a specific, potentially identifiable, agent. After Pasteur and Koch demonstrated in the nineteenth century that the introduction of specific virulent micro-organisms (i.e., germs) into the body produced specific diseases, one central focus of scientific medicine became the identification of these specific agents and the demonstration of their causal link with specific diseases. According to Dubos, although this doctrine has led to significant theoretical and practical achievements, it has seldom provided a complete understanding of disease causation. For example, he asks, why do only some people get sick some of the time, even though infectious agents are ubiquitous? Although the search for specific disease-producing agents was relatively successful for infectious diseases, it has proved too simplistic in explaining the causes of complex, chronic illnesses. Another undesirable byproduct of this assumption, according to Dubos, is the quest for a medicinal 'magic bullet' for each disease to 'shoot and kill' it, producing an over-emphasis upon pharmaceuticals in the 'armamentarium' (stock of weapons) of the modern doctor. Although some pharmaceutical intervention (e.g., the polio vaccine) has proven effective, Dubos' analysis suggests that greater health benefits would have been realized by investing societies' money and energy in public health measures and broader improvements in the social and physical environments of the populace.

One of the oldest Western images for understanding the body is the *machine metaphor* – another implicit assumption in modern medical knowledge. According to this metaphor, disease is the malfunctioning of some constituent mechanism (such as a 'breakdown' of the lungs). Other cultures use other metaphors: for example, ancient Egyptian societies used the image of a river, and Chinese tradition refers to the balance of elemental forces (Yin and Yang) of the earth (Osherson and Amarasingham 1981). Modern medicine has extended this image of the body as machine, emphasizing individual systems or organs to the exclusion of an image of the totality of the body. This machine metaphor encouraged an instrumentalist approach to the body, in which the role of the physician is to 'repair' the broken part.

Without denying the considerable achievements accomplished within this medical model, we might well question some of these assumptions upon which modern Western medicine is built. By rethinking the underpinnings of the healing enterprise, we might better meet the needs (including the biophysical needs) of the sick, we might be able to socialize more caring, person-oriented physicians, and we might glimpse how religion could be reintegrated into effective approaches to healing the whole person.

The relevance of religion for health and healing

Some recent developments suggest new appreciation for the linkage between religion and health. Although traditional religious responses to illness held some validity (and effectiveness) for their cultural setting, those wishing to reassert religion's role in healthcare and healing should not merely dust off old beliefs and practices. Rather, some creative new approaches are needed to address the health and healing needs of modern people in modern social contexts. The following discussion outlines a few approaches to a new appreciation of the potential for religion (and other nonmedical sources) to affect health and healing.

A new medical model

Even within some sectors of the medical enterprise, there is increasing interest in developing a new medical model – an approach to mind, body and society as being not merely linked but indeed interpenetrating in complex and, as yet, little-understood ways. Illnesses previously considered to be purely biogenic have been found to be related to social and psychological states, such as stress, conflict, sense of 'threat', role dissatisfaction, rapid social change, and sense of powerlessness. Some researchers suggest that stress and emotional distress influence the body through the effects of the central nervous system on the immunologic defences and possibly through the stress-responsive nervous system. Other researchers have noted that the impact of stress upon the body is mediated by the meaning the individual attaches to the stressful event. A growing medical and social-psychological literature argues that biophysical conditions are closely intertwined with a sense of well-being, mastery and harmony in one's social environment (for a concise review of the extensive literature on mind-body-society connections as they apply to health and healing, see Freund and McGuire 1991).

Some researchers have suggested that the 'placebo effect' should be taken more seriously, perhaps as evidence of the power of symbols to effect healing. Although the pharmaceutical placebo, for example, is not chemically effective, the individual may gain a real sense of being empowered by taking it (Moerman 1983). Religious rituals and symbols may impart a similar sense of empowerment to believers with concrete physical, as well as psychological, effects (McGuire 1988; Moerman 1979).

If some of these mind-body-society linkages are taken seriously, we can imagine the potential for a wide range of non-biophysical (including religious) approaches to promoting health and healing. In a more holistic model, for example, the social-emotional support offered by a family, religious group, or other personal network, could be not merely something done on the periphery but rather a central part of the healing process. Religious beliefs, prayer, meditation or ritual practices, and sense of community are potentially sources of greater well-being of the whole person (including the person's physical body).

If the individualistic bias of the present medical model were discarded, it would be possible to address the entire range of causes of illness, rather than to focus narrowly on purely physical causes. In an appalling number of cases, sick bodies are *socially* produced: through malnutrition and lack of basic public health measures (such as sewage treatment, safe housing and clean water); through environmental contamination, workplace hazards and unsafe products; through warfare, political torture, street violence and domestic abuse. Religious institutions are as well poised to address these social causes of illness as are medical institutions. If religion were applied to these issues, it could affect people's well-being far more directly than a medical system focused on treating individuals (as individual bodies) *after* their society has made them sick.

This approach would require raising the line of vision beyond the boundary of the body of the sick individual to the wider emotional and social contexts of illness (McKinlay 1986). So long as the 'problem' is located in the sick individual's body, treatment and prevention are addressed only to that individual body. There are some important (and perhaps uncomfortable) political and social policy implications in addressing the causes of illness and needs for well-being of the whole person.

Suffering and affliction

The experience of illness is distressing because it threatens the order and meanings by which people make sense of their lives. It threatens the ability to plan for the immediate or distant future, to control and to organize life. Illness, suffering and death raise questions of meaning, such as: Why is this happening to me? Why now? Who is responsible? How could God allow this to happen? Why do good people suffer while bad people prosper? and so on. Western medicine has difficulty dealing with sufferers' problems of meaning.

Cassell (1982: 639) notes that the reason biomedicine fails to deal adequately with people's distress is that suffering is 'experienced by persons, not merely by bodies, and has its sources in challenges that threaten the intactness of the person as a complex social and psychological entity'. As a result of the blinders implicit in the medical model, medical personnel often unknowingly cause suffering by failing to validate a patient's suffering, not acknowledging or responding to the personal meanings the patient attaches to the illness. Many people may seek help and healing primarily for suffering and affliction, and less for the disease itself (and for this reason they are often profoundly disappointed by medical treatment which identifies only the disease – if any – as the focus of treatment).

Cassell (1982: 642) states that 'people suffer from what they have lost of themselves in relation to the world of objects, events and relationships'. For example, one woman had suffered terribly from a hysterectomy she had undergone six years before our interview. Unmarried, childless and only twenty-nine years old, she had lost 'a huge part of [her] future'. Physicians and hospital staff may have considered her specific uterine problem to be the proper focus of their work and, insensitive to her suffering, had treated her 'like an ungrateful child, crying over spilt milk' (quoted in McGuire 1988).

Arguing the necessity of listening to, acknowledging and taking into account the meanings which sick people have for their suffering, Kleinman (1988: 26) states:

The cultural meanings of illness shape suffering as a distinctive moral or spiritual form of distress. Whether suffering is cast as the ritual enactment of despair, as paradigmatic moral exemplars of how pain and loss should be borne (as in the case of Job), or as the ultimately existential human dilemma of being alone in a meaningless world, local cultural systems provide both the theoretical framework of myth and the established script for ritual behaviour that transform the individual's affliction into a sanctioned symbolic form for the group.

Religion is potentially linked with healing by its ability to respond effectively to suffering and distress. It need not be merely a salve to soothe the afflicted (although that may be a valued function, too), but religion can be one source of a renewed sense of coherence in the person's world, restoring hurt links with loved ones, valued group ties, and lost social roles. In my research on spiritual approaches to healing (see McGuire 1988), respondents spoke impressively of being transformed and enlarged – not diminished – by the resolution of their illness experience.

Illness, distress and dissent

Anthropologists have noted that illness is often an idiom of distress by which the individual's body expresses a larger set of social and psychological concerns. For example, when an Iranian woman complains of a 'pressed heart', she may be simultaneously expressing distress over attractiveness, sexual intercourse, possible infertility, old age, or social pollution (Good 1977). Body symbolism is a pervasive and potent expression of larger individual or social meanings. Such idioms of distress in contemporary Western societies may include, for example, anorexia, ulcers, menopausal complaints, some heart problems, some respiratory problems, some chronic pain syndromes. To suggest that these problems are expressions of distress does not mean that they are not *also* physical and very real in the experience of the sufferer; it does mean, however, that any successful treatment must somehow address the sick person's real concerns, not merely the physical symptoms.

Illness may also be a way of expressing dissent and dissatisfaction about frustrated and unmet human needs. In effect, the sick person is saying, 'I will not any longer.' As such, claiming the sick role resembles the activist strategy of passive resistance. In the extreme, sickness is a refusal to cope, to struggle and to endure (Lock 1986). The medical response (and, often, also the religious response) has frequently been to individualize these expressions, denying their broader social sources.

Indeed, too often, the medical and religious response has been one of social control, suppressing the dissent and minimizing its impact. For example, it is very unlikely that either a medical or religious advisor, trying to help a woman with frequent headaches and 'attacks of nerves', would even 'hear' her accounts of her illness as expressions of dissent against a miserable work situation or oppressive family roles. Furthermore, rather than admit that her dissent may be justified (even though counter-productive), these contemporary advisors would be very likely to exercise social control to reduce her dissent and bring her back to closer conformity with social expectations, saying in effect 'You need to adjust yourself to the situation, and these Valium tablets (or inspirational messages and prayers) will help you feel better in the meantime.'

How different would be a medical or religious response that acknowledged some such dissent as justified! For example, working in an inner-city clinic, a young black internist from a middle-class background exclaimed:

The more I see, the more appalled I am at how ignorant I have been, insensitive to the social, economic and political causes of disease . . .

Today I saw an obese hypertensive mother of six. No husband. No family support. No job. Nothing. A world of brutalizing violence and poverty and drugs and teenage pregnancies and – and just plain mind-numbing crises, one after another after another . . . What is killing her is her world, not her body. In fact, her body is the product of her world. She is a hugely overweight, misshapen hulk who is a survivor of circumstances and lack of resources and cruel messages to consume and get ahead impossible for her to hear and not feel rage at the limits of her world. Hey, what she needs is not medicine but a social revolution (quoted in Kleinman 1988: 216–17).

Beyond its traditional function as a source of social control, religion can also serve to voice human rights and legitimate social dissent. Religious groups, as well as individual counsellors, can open their ears to the deeper sources of dissatisfaction and unhappiness. When illness is a metaphor for distress and dissent, religion can be a source of healing only if it acknowledges those meanings.

Bibliographical References

D. Callahan, *Setting Limits: Medical Goals in an Aging Society*, New York 1987.
D. Callahan, *What Kind of Life?: The Limits of Medical Progress*, New York 1989.
E. Cassell, 'The Nature of Suffering and the Goals of Medicine', *New England Journal of Medicine* 306, 1982, 639–45.
P. Conrad and J. Schneider, *Deviance and Medicalization: From Badness to Sickness*, St. Louis 1980.
R. Dubos, *The Mirage of Health*, Garden City, NY 1959.
E. Durkheim, *The Division of Labor in Society*, New York 1964 [1893].
G. Engel, 'The Need for a New Medical Model', *Science* 196, 1977, 129–36.
M. Foucault, *The Birth of the Clinic*, New York 1973.
E. Freidson, *Profession of Medicine*, New York 1970.
P. Freund and M. McGuire, *Health, Illness and the Social Body*, Englewood Cliffs, NJ 1991.
B. Good, The Heart of What's the Matter: The Semantics of Illness in Irán', *Culture, Medicine and Psychiatry* 1, 1977, 25–58.
D. Gordon, 'Tenacious Assumptions in Western Medicine', in *Biomedicine Examined*, ed. M. Lock and D. Gordon, Dordrecht 1988, 19–56.
R. Hann and A. Kleinman, 'Biomedical Practice and Anthropological Theory', *American Review of Anthropology* 12, 1983, 305–33.
L. Kirmayer, 'Mind and Body as Metaphors: Hidden Values in Biomedicine', in *Biomedicine Examined*, M. Lock and D. Gordon, Dordrecht 1988, 57–94.
A. Kleinman, *The Illness Narratives: Suffering, Healing, and the Human Condition*, New York 1988.
L. Levin and E. Idler, *The Hidden Health Care System: Mediating Structures and Medicine*, Cambridge, Mass. 1981.

M. Lock, 'Speaking "Truth" to Illness: Metaphor, Reification, and a Pedagogy for Patients', Paper presented to the American Anthropological Association 1986.

M. McGuire, *Ritual Healing in Suburban America*, New Brunswick, NJ 1988.

J. McKinlay, 'A Case for Refocusing Upstream: The Political Economy of Illness', in P. Conrad and R. Kern (eds.), *The Sociology of Health and Illness*, New York 1986, 484–98.

D. Moerman, 'Anthropology of Symbolic Healing', *Current Anthropology* 20, 1979, 59–66.

D. Moerman, 'Physiology and Symbols. The Anthropological Implications of the Placebo Effect', in L. Romanucci-Ross et al.(eds.), *The Anthropology of Medicine*, South Hadley, Mass. 1983, 156–67.

S. Osherson and L. Amarasingham, 'The Machine Metaphor in Medicine', in *Social Contexts of Health, Illness, and Patient Care*, E. Mishler et al., Cambridge 1981, 218–49.

M. Sullivan, 'In What Sense is Contemporary Medicine Dualistic?', *Culture, Medicine, and Psychiatry* 10, 1986, 331–50.

I. Zola, *Socio-Medical Inquiries*, Philadelphia 1983.

The Sacrament of Anointing: Open Questions

David N. Power

Most of the recent writing on the theology of the sacrament of the anointing of the sick followed in the wake of the Second Vatican Council or of the promulgation of the revised sacramental rite.[1] The Constitution on the Liturgy determined the direction which this interest took, by the simple statement that what had been usually called 'extreme unction' would be more fittingly called 'anointing of the sick'. Since it is not a rite intended for the point of death, 'as soon as anyone of the faithful begins to be in danger of death from sickness or old age, the fitting time to receive this sacrament has already arrived'.[2]

This was in sharp contrast with the position taken in the years preceding the Council by some prominent theologians, who presented the sacrament as an anointing for death, somehow paralleling the anointing which completes baptism at the beginning of the Christian life.[3] At the same time, however, the conciliar position had been prepared by historical studies on the various uses of blessed oil in early Christian centuries, and by examination of the euchology for the blessing of oils through the Middle Ages, which showed decided interest in bodily as well as in spiritual effects.[4]

In theological writings following the council, it was apparent that when writers employed the usual scholastic distinctions, four points needed consideration.[5] These were: the matter and form of the sacrament, its minister, the subjects for whose benefit it is intended, and its effects. On all of these points there is some variation in the discussion, and there are some matters which have not received recognition in the revision of the rite. Because of this, it may well be said that in the light of history and dogma there are some open questions the discussion of which could lead to further change in the ecclesial use of the sacrament of anointing. These points will be reviewed in this article, which will also offer a perspective in the light of which these issues take on a new appearance and are open to a truly ecclesial resolution.

1. Oils and their blessing

The apostolic constitution of Paul VI prescribing the revised rite for the sacrament made a number of significant changes with regard to the substance used and with regard to its actual use.[6] The words used in the anointing, and the action of anointing, were greatly simplified. They put less stress on the forgiveness of sins and were directed to the restoration of body and spirit, in keeping with the orientation of early Christian prayers. Allowance was also made for oils other than olive oil, which would be locally obtainable, according to place and climate.

More complex sacramental issues, however, emerged in relation to the fact that the proper matter of the sacrament is blessed oil. For centuries, the oil for this sacrament had been blessed by the bishop of the diocese on Maundy Thursday, along with the chrism and the oil of catechumens. It was also apparent that in centuries which allowed for self-ministration of the oil, or for the anointing of the sick by lay persons as well as presbyters, the one common factor had been the blessing of the oil by the bishop.[7]

On the other hand, the direction taken in the liturgical revision of rites after the Second Vatican Council was to restore a prayer of blessing to all sacraments, said in immediate conjunction with the offer of the sacrament to individual persons, following the model of the relation of the eucharistic prayer to the communion table. This had been followed out in the revision of the rites of baptism, which called for a blessing of water in immediate conjunction with baptismal immersion, even though this meant that Easter water would not always be used.[8] This, however, did not touch on the minister, since presbyters were in any case the usual ministers for the blessing of water. For the blessing of the oils of the sick, connecting the blessing directly with the celebration of the sacrament, meant that the ideal that the oils used always carry an episcopal blessing was renounced. The liturgy for Maundy Thursday retains a solemn blessing of oils for the anointing of the sick, along with the blessing of the chrism and the oil of catechumens. The ritual for the anointing of the sick is somewhat cautious on the score of using oils, already blessed, since it does not want to derogate from this annual action. On the other hand, in order not to limit the possibility of the sacrament in the absence of oils blessed by a bishop, it allows for a blessing by a presbyter.[9] Furthermore, in order to have a prayer of blessing with every anointing, whatever oil is used, the ritual prescribes that in using oils blessed by a bishop the presbyter should pray a prayer of thanksgiving similar to a prayer of blessing.[10]

A liturgical understanding of the nature of the traditional Jewish and Christian blessing prayer, with its anamnetic quality and its components of thanksgiving and intercession, shows that there is little difference in the ritual between the prayer called a blessing of the oils and the prayer called a thanksgiving over the blessed oils. Indeed, one may well ask whether the claim that this latter is not a blessing of oils already blessed is not a conceptual fiction that derives from a consecratory and rather material notion of blessing, alien to the thought that it is within the blessing of God by the church that the blessing of people and things in God's name occurs. It is also a conceptual fiction that avoids the close epicletic conjunction between the invocation of the Spirit upon persons and things simultaneously, rather than separately.[11] It is, however, a conceptual fiction that satisfies the more liturgically based desire to join anamnetic invocation of God with the actual anointing, without seeming to do violence to the more formal and juridical perception of episcopal powers and their effect.

Resort to this conceptual fiction shows up the anomaly of the current situation in regard to the material element of this sacrament. What is the point of the annual blessing of the oil of the sick by the bishop, and of carrying this oil once a year from the cathedral to the parishes of a diocese, if in the actual celebration of the sacrament another oil may be used, or a prayer of liturgical blessing is again to be prayed over oils blessed? There are actually two ministries involved, the episcopal and the presbyteral, and two occasions, the one the solemn diocesan ceremony and the other the celebration of the sacrament in the immediate interests of the sick. It is unsufficient to consider the matter in terms of sacramental power. In those terms, clearly it is thought that the presbyter has power to bless oils, as well as to anoint. Putting the matter in rather different terms, the issue is whether there is something ecclesially and sacramentally appropriate in connecting the care and sacrament of the sick with the pastoral ministry of bishops and with a solemn public celebration. If this is so, how can it be respected without resorting to a practice of the annual blessing of this oil, which is becoming more and more a simple formality, already deemed out of touch with the reality of the sacramental ministry to the sick and its appropriate celebration? Thus it appears that the apparently simple question of the matter to be used raises deeper sacramental and pastoral issues, that have to be addressed in a fuller ecclesial perspective.

2. The sacramental minister

Consideration of the blessing of the oil has already raised questions about the minister. More often, however, queries occur in the context of a need to make the actual anointing more generally accessible to the sick.[12]

Though little is known of practice in the early Christian centuries, tracing evidence found from the third century onward one can point to an evolution in three stages as far as the minister is concerned.[13] The first is that in which the blessing of oils is reserved to a bishop, but a wide variety of practice in the use of the oil is apparent. This included anointing by bishops, presbyters, deacons, or any one of the baptized, as well as self-administration. The oil was used to anoint the body or parts of the body, but it was also drunk or simply touched by the sick person. The second stage of development witnesses to the gradual reservation of the anointing to bishops and presbyters, though there is a wide variety of blessings and prayers and kinds of anointing. It was also during this period that its usage as extreme unction developed. This meant that forgiveness of sins and anointing were closely tied, especially in cases in which a dying penitent had not met the requirements of canonical penance. There is an obvious connection between this and the reservation of the sacrament to ordained priests. This is the stage of development that received dogmatic sanction from the Council of Trent and that perdured until the Second Vatican Council. The third stage of development was inaugurated by that council, in opening up the desire for a more regular celebration of the sacrament, not tied to the immediate danger of death.

Once that interest has been made manifest and translated into a revised ritual, the question of the minister naturally arises in new ways. If the sacrament is to be more readily available to the sick, in any situation of serious illness, is it necessary and proper to reserve anointing to priests, either bishops or presbyters? It was thus asked in post-conciliar theology whether anointing of the sick might be extended to deacons, and even to baptized faithful, particularly those now authorized to celebrate baptism, preside at communion services, officiate at marriages and bury the dead. Given the importance which the new rite gives to the blessing of the oil, the question would stretch to the possible right of such persons to bless the oil for the sick.

In discussing the appropriate minister, three historical factors have been given consideration. The first has to do with the identity of the *presbyteroi* in the text of James 5.15.[14] It seems that they are persons holding some official position in the church as its leaders, though one can hardly say whether they had received office through a laying-on of hands, given the vague state of the question about induction into church office in New Testament times. Those who argue that at least some among the baptized are called on to anoint the sick, would say that it is not the particular identity of the elders that counts, but the communal and public nature of the prayer and anointing, which distinguishes this rite from charismatic healing or from some private use of oils.

The second historical factor deemed of importance is the widespread practice of lay-anointing in earlier epochs. In arguing from this, however, it has to be noted that the blessing of oil was done by the bishop and that there were different degrees of solemnity in the use of the blessed oil, and obviously differences in the rites and prayers used. Only a narrow idea of sacrament, expressed in terms of matter and form, would identify the sacrament with any and every use of oil, some hardly distinguishable from a rather common use of blessed water. The question about the ministry of the baptized in the anointing of the sick has to be addressed in the full liturgical context of an accredited and duly celebrated church ministry. Allowing all the faithful to bring home oil for use, in a manner similar to the use of blessed water, might be a good thing, but it is not to be confounded with the celebration of the sacrament, nor should it lead to the perfunctory dabbing with oils. The question today needs to be sharply phrased as one that has to do with calling on the baptized to officiate in solemn liturgical rites, whether in church, in hospitals or in homes, in the anointing of the sick. The principal argument in favour of this is the pastoral availability, to individual sick and to whole communities, of the celebration of this sacrament.

Hence the third historical factor has to be addressed, namely, the intent of the Council of Trent in defining that the proper minister of the sacrament is an ordained priest, bishop or presbyter.[15] The departure from the common usage in the use of the word 'proper' instead of 'ordinary' minister in canon 4 of the decree has been noted. It is argued that Trent's principal intention in the matter was to defend the efficacy and divine institution of this sacrament against the Reformers, and to associate it with the normal and usual sacramental ministry of ordained priests. If there was no direct and professed intention to settle the question of the minister once and for all, this would of course leave open the possibility for further discussion and eventual change in the practice of the church.

Within the present policy of the Western church concerning candidacy for ordination, it is difficult to avoid treating this issue as part of an emergency situation in which many communities of faith are left without ordained ministers, and hence without the full range of sacramental celebration. The least that can be said is that in present circumstances, and given the state of the church's tradition, it appears appropriate and justified to extend the faculty to celebrate the sacrament of the sick to baptized persons who officiate already as ministers of communion, baptism, marriage and funerals. Beyond that, it could also be argued that there are other situations, hardly considered situations of emergency, in which baptized faithful might well be considered appropriate ministers of the sacrament. Here one might think of hospitals, or home visitation, where baptized persons exercise a spiritual and healing ministry to the sick as a regular matter. They might well be the ones most fitted to complete this pastoral ministry with the celebration of the sacrament, always being careful not to reduce it to a perfunctory rubbing with oil and muttering of a formula. Theologically and pastorally, nothing is gained by allowing others to do badly what priests already do badly.

3. The Subject

In suggesting the adoption of the name 'anointing of the sick' to complement, and even replace, 'extreme unction', the Second Vatican Council opened its administration to a wider range of persons. At the same time, it wished to keep alive the sense that the celebration of the sacrament supposed a certain gravity in illness and even retained some mention of the danger of death. The *Ordo Unctionis Infirmorum* omits the direct mention of death, but states that the sacrament is for those '*qui propter infirmitatem vel senium periculose aegrotant*'.[16]

Much discussion has gone into the meaning of the adverb *periculose*.[17] The official Italian translation of the rite uses a nice circumlocution, speaking of the faithful whose state of health is seriously compromised, either by illness or by old age.[18] What is excluded in the discussion is the notion that there has to be an imminent danger of death. At the same time, despite some vagueness on how widely the sacrament may be used, it is thought to pertain to illness that carries a considerable degree of difficulty and danger. In this connection, it ought to be noted that the *Ordo* envisages the celebration of the sacrament not only in homes and sick rooms, but also in public churches, with the gathering of all the faithful, so that the sacrament becomes a true ecclesial and communal liturgy.[19] Though this does not touch directly on the subject of the sacrament, it carries some connotation of persons not only brought, but even going themselves, to church, as well as a rather broad invitation to sick persons to present themselves.

The most pertinent observation on this score is probably one made by

Giorgio Gozzelino.[20] He points out that while the sacrament is for the physically ill, and may well have some physical effects, it is a celebration of faith and is intended for the spiritual strength of the sick, in face of their debility and danger. Hence, he suggests, the proper criterion concerning apt subjects may not be in the physical order at all but in the spiritual. That is to say, the sacrament is for those who, being clinically ill, undergo serious spiritual crisis, making it difficult for them to sustain faith and hope, and to live human life with resolution and dignity. What would affect one person seriously in this sense might not disturb another, and it is not possible to judge the opportuneness of the sacrament by considering only the physical condition of the ill or elderly.

This is a good counterpoint to the tendency to act or write as though the decision to celebrate the sacrament were to be made by person or persons other than the sick themselves. Some discussion in the 1960s and 1970s touched on border-line cases, such as the elderly in no proximately foreseeable danger of death but impeded by old age, the handicapped, the mentally ill, and sick children not yet of communion age. At the same time, theologians were looking for a more general principle, within whose orbit such cases might be considered. If the weakness which endangers the person's living is not simply physical but psychosomatic, then it is the subject's personal disposition which is the decisive factor. This means that, as in the general principle for all sacraments, the initiative in asking for the anointing of the sick belongs to the subject. It is the sick person who has to judge whether or not the sacrament would be beneficial to faith and human wholeness. Granted that in a few of the particular cases mentioned, such as the mentally handicapped or small children, the initiative would often come from another person, by and large one can take the disposition and decision of the subject as conclusive. Even in the exceptional cases just mentioned, parents or guardians would have to discern whether the ill person would be able to participate in some measure of personal faith in the rites of anointing.

4. The effects

The discussions about extending the ministry of anointing and about the persons to be anointed make it clear that the principal theological and pastoral issue is the effect of the sacrament. How is it intended to benefit participation in the paschal mystery of Christ, and what grace accrues to sick persons from this participation?

By reason of the mediaeval developments in the administration of the sacrament which led it to be considered as extreme unction, the reception of anointing was very closely linked with the forgiveness of sins. Even the formula in the Roman Ritual of 1614 highlighted this effect.[21] At the same time, the church insisted that serious sin had to be remitted by the sacrament of penance. Hence, theologians discussed the exact meaning of the forgiveness offered through extreme unction, ranging between removal of the remainder of sin, the remission of venial sins, and strength to resist the temptations that come with the imminence of death. On the other hand, with the Council of Trent they were unable to bypass the issue of bodily effects,[22] though this was listed as something secondary and occasional.

It is apparent that the question cannot be left in strictly classical form, with the attempt to enumerate the graces and other benefits that accrue to the individual when the sacrament is administered. This was already evident to those theologians who in the period preceding the Second Vatican Council wrote of extreme unction as an anointing for death. Their intention was to give it a positive meaning and to present it as a participation in the pasch and worship of Jesus Christ.

It is indeed fundamental to reflect on the relation of human suffering and sickness to the paschal mystery of Christ and to ask what promise Christ's death and resurrection hold out to the ill. In limiting the use of the sacrament to those in proximate danger of death, these theologians did not do justice to the sacrament's bodily effect. With the retrieval of an earlier history and the change in formulation of the Second Vatican Council, this has been given much more consideration.

However, it is done in such a way as to relate it primarily to faith and participation in Christ's pasch, rather than to see it as an instance of charismatic healing. At the same time, there is no wish to abandon the connection with the forgiveness of sins, something which is already mentioned in the letter of James which serves as biblical foundation to this sacrament.

In keeping with the general renewal of sacramental theology, writers also attempt to retrieve the ecclesial dimension of anointing. To do this, they place it in relation to the church's total ministry to the sick and consider the place which the sick have in the church as a community of faith, that lives by Christ's Spirit in the hope of his pasch. In its attention to the sick the church faces the enigma of human suffering in the faith of Christ, assures them of its care and support, and by that same token in Christ's name guarantees them the strength and alleviation of the Spirit.

These orientations give rise to two principal sets of consideration. The first has to do with a phenomenology of human illness, concentrating more on the psychosomatic than on the purely physical conditions of being ill.[23]

The second, following on this, has to do with the pertinence of Christ's paschal victory to human illness and suffering. It should be noted that both of these considerations, anticipated in post-conciliar theological writing, were given place in the introduction to the revised ritual for the pastoral care of the sick. This introduction pointed out that anointing allows the church, and the sick in particular, a specific participation in the paschal mystery, in which Christ overcame all evil and opened the way to the fullness of life in the Spirit. It also pointed out that as an expression of eschatological hope, the sacrament belongs in the context of the church's ministry and of the human effort to overcome illness and its consequences, even while in this present time there is a necessary share in Christ's sufferings.[24]

The aim of the phenomenology of human illness offered in theological writing on the sacrament is ultimately to see how strengthening of faith, acceptance of suffering without loss of resolution, bodily alleviation and overcoming of sin, converge in the sick person's participation in the paschal mystery. The key word in describing the state of being ill, rather than the purely physical reality, is alienation. In illness, the human person experiences a multiple estrangement, from one's own body, from friends and associates, from the doings of society, and from God. Sin as a global reality, rather than simply as personal offence, has a hold on the person through this alienation. The spirit is weakened by the bodily condition, and conversely weakness of spirit makes the effort to deal with the bodily condition difficult. As the evil to be overcome resides in this multiple alienation, so the grace of the sacrament, shared with the community in faith, is granted for the alleviation of this condition. The traditional categories of grace, forgiveness of sin and bodily effect can all be subsumed into this more comprehensive and more focused perception of illness and its alleviation. It is a viewpoint which moreover allows for the difference in effect from case to case, given that neither the physical nor the spiritual condition is identical in any two sick persons.

In expressing the grace of the sacrament as that of alleviating the person in the midst of illness, theological writing relates it to the paschal mystery. The main force of the sacrament is to allow the sick to participate in this mystery, in a way appropriate to the condition of being sick. It is to permit the person to live the mystery in sickness and to live this condition, rather than simply endure it, as a share in the mystery. Happily the introduction of epiclesis into the liturgical rite puts this in perspective. It is the grace of the eschatological Spirit, the first fruits of the pasch and the guarantor of its fullness, which is invoked upon the sick.[25] In receiving the Spirit, they receive the power which strengthens them in their present efforts and in the hope of Christ's final victory. They are enabled to be witnesses in the community, to faith and to hope and to the deeper qualities of the human. Their role as Christians, whether in their own lives or in the community, is not a passive one. In this connection it needs to be remarked that the one thing unfortunately lacking in the revised rite is the opportunity for the sick to give voice to their witness, either by word of encouragement, or by blessing invoked upon God and upon their human companions.

5. An Ecclesial Ritual and Sacrament

Eventually an adequate pastoral approach to the use of the sacrament of anointing can be worked out only if it is possible to regain the truly ecclesial nature of the sacrament, releasing it from an individualistic approach. This would make it possible to place the fullness of the sacrament in a common celebration. At the same time it could be linked with attendant rituals, which might well include a more variable use of blessed oils.

When the concern is too narrowly focused on giving the benefits of the sacrament as often as possible to the sick, a wide understanding of the state of illness is fostered, from which follows the appeal to allow its administration by persons other than priests (bishop or presbyter). While the ministry of all the baptized has to be given full consideration, in keeping with what has been said above, the risk is that of bypassing a fuller understanding of sacrament, and hence the questions appropriate to the full celebration of anointing as an ecclesial act of worship.

No sacrament is intended simply to confer grace on an individual. It is always a celebration of the pasch of Christ by the believing community, in relation to some aspect of the offer of salvation and in relation to the needs of particular individuals in the community. It is for the whole church, and is an invitation to the church's deepening of faith and its praise of God. The offer of salvation in Christ's name, within the community of faith, is concretized in the persons of those for whom a particular grace is asked of God, in the faith of what is proclaimed.

All of this means that the use of anointing has its centre in a community assembly, in which the full form of sacramental celebration is respected. In earlier church times it is likely that this was guaranteed by the blessing of the oils by the bishop within a community gathering, especially when this was closely related to the annual celebration of Christ's death and resurrection. The episcopal blessing of oils, however, rarely has that part in the church nowadays, whatever the efforts have been to restore it to the status of a diocesan celebration, in the days coming towards the end of Lent. Today the community nature of the blessing would be better assured within a parish celebration, or in a hospital chapel with family and friends in attendance, held at appropriate times, such as Advent, Lent or Paschaltide, when the relation to the mystery of Christ would stand out within the context of the liturgical calendar. Around this central service, a number of ritual usages could grow up, in various degrees of solemnity, inclusive of presbyteral, diaconal and lay anointing. In such rituals, care needs to be taken that the anointing, however simple, is always done in the context of word and prayer, not being reduced to a perfunctory dabbing.

This is to espouse a notion of the sacramental which sees each of the seven sacraments as having a core, complemented by several integral parts. These offer a participation in the sacrament and fill out the place which the sacrament has in the life of the church and of the individual faithful. The model for this understanding and usage is the revised order for adult initiation into the church. While the paschal immersion and chrismation, with admission to the communion table, is at the heart of this celebration, it is lacking in insight not to see how the rites before and after this night are an integral part of the sacrament. They flow as it were from it and take their meaning from it, but also fill out its efficacious celebration, so that it is incomplete without them. During the 1983 Synod on Penance and Reconciliation a number of bishops expressed an understanding of penance similar to this.[26]

While allowing that there is a core part of the sacrament (not at all identified in a satisfactory way by the Synod and post-synodal documents), they saw how other actions and rites could foster penance and reconciliation in relationship to this. Thus private confession, either to a priest or to one of the baptized faithful, as well as communal word services, could relate to a core moment of community celebration, in virtue of which all these concordant rites and actions have their meaning and their place in the paschal communion of the church. Something similar takes place surrounding a community celebration of the anointing of the sick, complete with proclamation of the word and the blessing of oil. It flows over into a further use of the oils in other situations, as indeed into other ritual actions, such as a laying-on of hands in a sick room, where two or three are gathered in Christ's name.

Conclusion

Many questions have been raised by the position taken on the sacrament of the sick by the Vatican Council. There are helpful orientations in theological writing, but not all the questions are uniformly answered. What counts most of all at present is to reclaim the anointing of the sick as a sacrament of the church, and to find in this the best response to the needs of the sick and to their sustenance in faith. This is not done by insisting that the priest is minister, but by allowing an enlarged use of oils within a context where attention is paid to a community celebration in which the word is proclaimed, the oils are blessed, the sick are anointed, and all share together in the body and blood of Christ. Only in this way will there be a full integration of issues of human sickness and health into a redemptive economy, with due attention both to ecclesial reality and individual need.

Notes

1. *Ordo Unctionis Infirmorum eorumque Pastoralis Curae*, editio typica, Vatican City 1972.
2. The Second Vatican Council, *Constitution on the Liturgy*, no. 73.
3. Some of the principal examples are Karl Rahner, Alois Grillmeier and Michael Schmaus. These positions are reviewed in Basil Studer, 'Letzte Ölung oder Krankensalbung', *Freiburger Zeitschrift für Philosophie und Theologie* 10, 1963, 33–60.
4. A most influential study was that of Antoine Chavasse, *Du IIIe, siècle à la réforme carolingienne. Etudes sur l'onction des infirmes dans l'église latine du IIe, au XIe siècle*, Lyons 1942.
5. Some of the major studies, each including ample reference to periodical literature, are: Gioregio Gozzelino, *L'Unzione degli Infermi, Sacramento della Vittoria sulla Malattia*, Turin 1970; José Luis Larrabe, *La Iglesia y el Sacramento de la Unción de los Enfermos*, Salamanca 1974; Claude Ortemann, *Le Sacrament des Malades*, Lyons 1971; Herbert Vorgrimler, *Büsse und Krankensalbung*, Freiburg im Breisgau 1978.
6. Paul VI, *Constitutio Apostolica de Sacramento Unctionis Infirmorum*, 1972, reprinted in the editio typica of the ritual.
7. Most commonly cited is the letter of Innocent I to Decentius of Gubbio. Cf. DS 216.
8. Cf. no. 21 of the general norms on baptism, in *Ordo Baptismi Parvulorum*, editio typica, Vatican City 1969: '*Optandum vero est ut, extra tempus Paschae, aqua pro singulis celebrationibus benedictione donetur, ut ipsis consecrationis verbis clare significetur salutis mysterium, quod Ecclesia recolit atque proclamat.*'
9. *Ordo Unctionis*, nos. 21 and 75.
10. Ibid., no. 75bis.
11. Cf. Jean-Marie Tillard, 'Blessing, Sacramentality and Epiclesis', *Concilium* 178, 1985, 96–110.
12. Cf. J.-C. Didier, 'Sur le ministre de l'onction des malades', *L'Ami du Clergé* 74, 1964, 488–92; Philippe Rouillard, 'Le ministre du sacrement de l'onction des malades', *Nouvelle Revue Théologique* 111, 1979, 395–402; A. Ziegenhaus, 'Ausdehnung der Spendevollmacht de Krankensalbung', *Münchener Theologische Zeitschrift* 26, 1975, 345–63.
13. A good summary of liturgical history is given by Achille Triacca, 'La Chiesa e i malati: "fedeltà" a Cristo e "adattamento" alle nuove situazioni storiche', in *Il Sacramento dei Malati*, Quaderni di Rivista Liturgica, no. 2, Turin 1975, 58–74.
14. Cf. B. Reicke, 'L'onction des malades d'après Saint Jacques', *La Maison-Dieu* 113, 1973, 50–6.

15. Cf. André Duval, 'L'extrême-onction au Concile de Trente', *La Maison-Dieu* 191, 1970, 127–72.
16. *Ordo Unctionis*, no. 8.
17. Cf. Table Ronde, 'A qui doit-on donner l'onction des malades?', *La Maison-Dieu* 113, 1973, 82–102.
18. 'il cui stato di salute risulta seriamente compromesso per malattia o vecchiaia.'
19. *Ordo Unctionis*, nos. 80–82.
20. Gozzelino, *Unzione*(n.5), 157–61.
21. '*Per istam sanctam unctionem et suam piissimam misericordiam indulgeat tibi Dominus quidquid . . . deliquisti.*'
22. Decree, chapter 2: DS 1696.
23. The thought of Ortemann, *Sacrament* (n.5), has had considerable repercussions.
24. *Ordo Unctionis*, nos. 5–7, 32–34.
25. On the epiclesis, cf. E. J. Lengeling, '*Per istam sanctam unctionem . . . adiuvet te Dominus gratia Spiritus Sancti*: der heilige Geist und die Krankensalbung', *Lex orandi, lex credendi. Miscellanea in onore di Cipriano Vagaggini*, Rome 1982, 235–94.
26. Cf. *Concilium* 190, 1987, *The Fate of Confession*, especially Catherine Dooley, 'The 1983 Synod of Bishops and the Crisis of Confession', 1–20, and David Power, 'Editorial Conclusions', 127–31.

Women, Healing Rituals and Popular Medicine in Mexico

Sylvia Marcos

After Mariana, age 60, completed these activities (preparing the temple), which were routine on healing days, she put on her long, spotless white robe. The other three women, ranging in age from 30 to 60, removed their white robes from the shopping bags and followed Mariana's example. As they were putting them on, I saw ordinary-looking women being transformed into repositories of power, capable of summoning spirits, and into experts for whose ministrations many people waited to entrust themselves (K. Finkler, *Spiritualist Healers in Mexico*, 1985).

Introduction

In pre-Columbian Mexico, healing always took place surrounded by prayer, invocations and sacred objects in a context that was explicitly religious. Today, healing rituals are most often carried out in the context of contemporary popular religion. There they reflect a relationship with the cosmos that is strongly marked by ancient beliefs. Current forms of healing may primarily recall tradition or may emerge from the fusion of cultures brought about by the Spanish conquest and subsequent colonization. Either way, popular medicine partakes of the cosmology that dominated Meso-American* cultures for millennia and still provides the implicit

*Note: Meso-America stretches from about half-way between the Central Mexican highlands and the United States border through Mexico and Guatemala, reaching into parts of El Salvador, Honduras and Nicaragua. The information concerning cosmology and popular medicine applies to this region as well as northern Mexico and even to Mexican-American populations that retain these influences.

knowledge system for many present-day healing procedures (Marcos 1988).

Underlying that cosmology was a pervasive concept of duality, of female and male. There were many important goddesses, and most deities had a feminine and masculine aspect. The cosmic force identified with the feminine was complemented by its male-identified counterpart. Women and men were profoundly influenced to view themselves, their interactions and functions in society as different but complementary on all levels and in all areas of life. Women healers expressed a world view in which they and the female aspect of life were integral to society. Further, accounts from the sixteenth and seventeenth centuries suggest that women outnumbered men as practitioners of the healing arts in pre-Columbian times. Today, it is within popular medicine that we see women healers acting in ways that take them beyond the roles imposed by their social and cultural context. The historical and ethnographic material reviewed below will indicate the range of healing activities performed by women and suggest the importance of their participation.

1. Popular medicine

Women's role in healing in Mexico is directly related to the nature of popular medicine, which includes its social functions and the knowledge system it is based upon. When we look at current popular medical practices, we see a deeply complex and many-layered whole that is outside but concurrent with mainstream medicine. As both a living, self-renewing tradition and the repository of pre-Columbian healing methods, values and world views, 'popular medicine' covers all curing actions outside formal, institutional, mainstream medicine. It includes most of the healing methods of the 'popular' classes. Its practitioners are almost exclusively of urban poor, peasant and indigenous origin, but those who seek healing, while most often of the same class, may come from any social background. People resort to *curanderismo* or popular medicine both as a first choice and after mainstream medicine has failed them.

'*Curanderismo*' is a Spanish term for a variety of healing practices and rituals (sometimes termed 'shamanistic' by foreign researchers). It defines a privileged realm where indigenous ethnicity entrenched itself and managed not only to survive the conquest, but became a focus for continuing, autonomous invention (Bonfil 1984). Elements from different historical periods fuse, are reorganized and recycled by the agents of this process: the large disadvantaged majorities who live in Mexico's urban centres and peasant communities.

In these communities it is often the *curandera* rather than the modern medical doctor who re-establishes the multi-dimensional equilibrium upset by 'sickness'. (*'Curandera/curandero'* is the term used for these healers. Since the majority are women, *'curandera'* will be used.) The *curandera* is, literally, a *'med – dicus'* in the classic sense of one who knows how to pronounce (*dicere*) the measure (Indo-European root: *med*) suitable to restore balance. 'Health', we will recall, is related to 'whole' through the Greek *'holos'*. To understand the deeper meaning of healing in these communities requires submersion in the largely Meso-American cosmology which is its source.

Currently among the Otomis of the Sierra Madre Oriental there exists an:

homology between the vision of the body and that of the universe . . . The Otomi concept of sickness reveals a series of concepts that are shown to be identical to those that orient their vision of the world, . . . the sickness localized in the body cannot be separated in certain form from disorder at a cosmic level (author's translation, Galinier 1986).

The integration of body and universe means that healing can only be conceived of in cosmological terms.

Gathering the information

Two concerns dominated the evolution of the method used to research the role of women in popular medicine. First, it was necessary to understand the context in which they operated. The conceptual framework underlying traditional medicine is like a woven fabric of which we have intriguing fragments, but not the overall pattern. Recovering it requires a kind of anamnesis which allows us to propose the missing elements of a conceptual weave. One of the ways to recover 'lost fragments' is by interviewing *curanderas* who are deeply rooted in their traditions or who have received a spiritual and mystical initiation and to compare their information with the oldest available accounts.

This in itself presented a challenge. The study of the *curanderas'* many recipes for teas and poultices, of prayers, imprecations, invocations, precepts for behaviour, and all the range of instructions to the sick for taking potions, protecting oneself from 'bad airs', envy and the evil eye can, at first sight, seem like the 'Chinese taxonomy' of Borges that made Foucault laugh. It is only gradually that some elements begin to emerge and even they, at first, can seem profuse, disconnected, bereft of interrelationship. This is precisely when we must fend off the temptation to discard as merely 'magical practices' what we cannot comprehend.

The second concern was to understand a healer at work. Answering this concern required extensive contact with and observation of *curanderas*. These contemporary experiences would then 'resonate' with and clarify the descriptions of healing rituals found in texts dating from the conquest and colonial periods.

One particular element of traditional *curanderismo* that became evident through interviews and is confirmed by other investigators is the importance of the tie with the divine in healing. At times the symbolic and ritual significance of popular healing is minimized. Much research on traditional medicine in Mexico attempts to demonstrate the 'scientific' basis for the ancient medical paradigms by proving the chemical effect-iveness of the plants involved and by emphasizing their similarity to modern pharmacological compounds. In another article I question this research strategy, calling it a 'formalistic fallacy'. Based on the belief that only modern scientific forms have validity, it implies that to gain respect for traditional medicine, we ought to study how it anticipated the contemporary institutional medical paradigm (Viesca 1984: Marcos 1988). Sellers of medicinal plants in Cuernavaca, Tepoztlan and Mexico City have a profound knowledge of the physical effects of their plants on various illness, but they insist that prayer is the absolutely essential element of the plants' healing power.

Finally, since we are dealing with the forced association of two cultures, the question occurs of how they merged to produce contemporary society. It is not a synthesis, but a dynamic process that comes closer to an interpenetration of civilizations that continues today (Bastide 1978). Within this dynamic process, we find elements reflecting pre-Hispanic cosmology, early Spanish medicine in its scientific and popular forms, and even the influence of institutional medicine. Contemporary popular medicine is thus the product of a permanent process of synthesis and appropriation of cultural elements. Key among these elements is a world view that places the feminine on a complementary basis with the masculine in the running and maintenance of the universe.

II. Cosmology

Popular medicine as practised in Meso-America is fed by the deep and powerful streams of ancient cosmology and concepts of European origin introduced by Spanish colonizers. These elements live an underground yet impressively vital existence, nourishing, especially, the healing practices and religious forms they belong to. However, there are no purely Aztec or purely Spanish elements making up these perceptions, images, influences and ideas which form the conceptual framework within which the majority of people in Meso-America face life and death. What is instructive and surprising is how they have persisted through the centuries despite ideas of progress and modern means of communication.

Presence of the feminine in the Meso-American pantheon

Basic to the cosmology that survived and continues to shape its participants is the feminine-masculine duality which is responsible for the creation of the cosmos, its regeneration and its maintenance. 'What these Indians understood as Divine Nature . . . (was) divided into two gods (known as) Man and Woman . . . ' (Torquemada, quoted by Leon Portilla, 1963).

A recurring feature of Meso-American thinking was the fusion of feminine and masculine into a singular, polar principle which was reflected in a pantheon where the divinities were conceptualized in pairs. Manuscripts from the sixteenth century testify to these concepts (Garibay 1959). The Mother and Father, Tonacatecutli-Tonacacihautl, and their creation: Uxumoco and Cipactonal; the gods of water: Tlaltecutli and his wife Chalchiuhtlicue, etc. Primary sources show the divine principle divided into numerous pairs; for example, Ometeotl-Omecihuatl, the god who is two, demonstrates the principle of complementaries. This double deity lived at Omeyocan, the place of duality. In the lower regions of the earth lived Mictlantecuhtli-Mictecacihuatl, the pair of gods who permitted access to the nine cosmic levels of the underworld (Sahagun 1956).

The feminine as a cosmic force was not a presence that imposed itself on its opposite, nor did it invalidate the masculine, try to negate it or make it appear secondary and subordinate to it. The feminine presence encompassed the masculine, went towards the masculine opposite and, in an eternal alternation, travelled between both definitions and was both at the same time. On the level of image, there were goddesses who at times appeared masculine or androgynous, as they have sometimes been interpreted. The concept of dual unity was found throughout all of Meso-America. Thus, Thompson spoke of Itzam Na and his partner Ix Chebel Yax in the Maya region (1975). Las Casas mentions Izona and his wife, and Diego de Landa refers also to Itzam Na and Ixchel as the gods of medicine (1967, 1960).

Feminine functions were divinized: Chantico, fire goddess of the earth; Chalchihuitlicue, female principle of fertility and goddess of lakes, rivers and springs; the four Izcuiname who support the cosmos at its four angles; Tlazolteotl, goddess of that which is cast off and of confession (an important ritual for pre-Columbian societies); the Cihuateteo, goddesses who help the sun descend from the zenith to sunset; Coatlicue, 'serpent skirt', giver of life and mother of the gods; Xochiquetzal, mother goddess of flowers; Xilonen, mother goddess of corn, and so on.

A multiple, fluid universe

Goddesses, however, were not personified as discrete entities and, given that the divine reality was multiple, fluid and encompassing of everything, their aspects were changing, their images dynamic, never fixed but continuously recreated and redefined. During brief moments in the constant shifting and flow, a goddess or god could be conceptualized (Hunt 1977).

In that fluid, dual universe the domain of the sacred was all pervasive. Continuity existed between the natural and supernatural world. Its sacred beings were closely interconnected with humans whose activity created interdependence. Failure to fulfil religious obligations could provoke divine anger and punishment. But the deities also needed worshippers, sacrifice, ritual and food (Leon Portilla 1963; Vogt 1976). This mutual interdependence was a matter of life and death for both the divine beings and the humans who adored them. Evidently this is a very particular sense of the sacred. The relationship is not with an all-powerful being who is eternally benevolent and powerful, beyond the good or bad deeds of devotees and independent of their rituals. For the Aztecs and other Indian groups, God was both the one and the many.

In the same vein, the divine included the earth, sky, clouds, rain, seeds, plants. Since the divine reality was multiple, fluid, encompassing the whole, its images were changing images, dynamic, never fixed but in a process of constant recreation and redefinition as the mystery of the nature of divinity itself.

As much as God was not an individuated entity, pre-Columbian peoples did not have the conceptual framework of full personal responsibility nor the Christian concept of the person (Andrews and Hassig 1984; Gruzinski 1988). Collectives – community, town, *Calpulli* (neighborhood), extended family and ritual networks – were the main sources of identity for Meso-Americans. In another work, I have analysed the difficulties the Indians had in understanding the concept of sin within the church's framework of free will and individual responsibility (Marcos 1989a).

The concept of the devil shocked the Aztec mind. Personifications of evil were as alien to the Indian mind as the personification of God. Aztec thought was fluid and characterized by changing rather than rigid or fixed dualities. The supernatural forces represented as gods and goddesses shifted continuously between the two poles of good and evil. They could protect and help or they could harm and destroy. The concept of a separate, all-beneficent entity was as unfamiliar as an all-evil one.

The merging and overlapping of divine images, which sometimes discourages linear-thinking researchers from making sense out of the primary sources and materials from Aztec cosmology, does not reflect an 'unfinished' pantheon. Rather, it was its very nature. The Aztecs and other Meso-American societies were neither monotheistic nor polytheistic. In their view, reality, nature and experience were nothing but multiple manifestations of a single unity of being (Hunt 1977).

It was within this cosmology with its duality, fluidity, divinized feminine presences and all-pervasive deity that the *curanderas* and other Mexican healers of the past moved and worked. The following accounts, one undertaken to record and the other to eradicate traditional beliefs, reveal the significance of the *curanderas* in their social settings.

III. *Curanderas* of the Past

Born in Spain around 1500, Fray Bernardino de Sahagun, a Franciscan, came to Mexico in 1529. Some ten years later he began travelling to gather material for his *General History of Things in New Spain*. Called the father of modern ethnology, Sahagun drew up a questionnaire that enabled him systematically to inventory much of the culture. Despite his critical comments about native religious beliefs, his extremely comprehensive accounts are regarded as one of the most reliable sources.

Female images in the Meso-American pantheon offer a vision of women's social functions revealed through their medical functions. Sahagun speaks of Temazcaltoci, calling her the goddess of medicine. Also the patron of the temazcal, the healing vapour bath, she was the 'heart of the earth and our grandmother; . . . doctors, surgeons and bleeders venerate her as well as the diviners who foretell the good or bad fortune that children will have according to their birth' (*Florentine Codex:* Book 1, Ch. VIII).

In his first encounter with this female healing power, Sahagun recorded the activities of what he called female doctors or *Titici* (*Ticitl* in singular):

> The female doctor knows well the properties of herbs, roots, trees and rocks. She has a great deal of experience with them and likewise knows many medical secrets. She who is a good doctor knows how to cure the sick, and, for the good which she does them, practically brings the dead back to life, making them get better or recover with the cures she uses. She knows how to bleed, to give purges, administer medicine and apply

ointments to the body, to soften lumps in the body by massage, to set bones, lance and cure wounds and the gout, cut away bad flesh and cure the evil eye.

. . . (By) blowing on the sick, subtly tying and untying cords, looking into water, throwing the large grains of corn customarily used in divination . . . she learns about and understands illnesses . . . (*Florentine Codex:* Book X, Ch. XIII).

Midwifery has traditionally been women's specialty, but additionally, in the Aztec world, midwives presided as priestesses at the rituals surrounding birth. They encouraged women on the battlefield of birth. Midwives directed the process, gave messages, prayed, administered herbs and took the women to the temazcal bath. Their duties included preparing pregnant women to become 'Cihuateteo', the goddesses that accompanied the sun from its height to its setting. If the mother were to die in childbirth, she would then become one of these goddesses. She was regarded the same as a warrior who dies on the battlefield.

. . . And when the baby arrived on earth, the midwife shouted; she gave war cries, which meant that the woman had fought a good battle, had become a brave warrior, had taken a captive, had captured a baby (Sahagun 1969).

Treatise on the Heathen Superstitions
After nearly 100 years of catechization, church authorities in colonial Mexico saw that native religious practices still persisted and even flourished. The church's official position when confronted with the complex, highly evolved religious system and beliefs of the New World's inhabitants was to attribute them to the devil. For Christians there was only one God, so the native deities – perceived by the catechizers as real and effective – must be evil spirits. Accordingly the religious customs and acts, which included ritual bathing and naming four days after birth, confessing (to the goddess Tlzolteotl), eating figures of the gods fashioned from amaranth, as well as other rituals that superficially recalled church practices, were regarded as attempts by the devil to lead souls astray by imitating Christian practices.

The effort to eliminate native religious customs focussed on bringing to judgment their practitioners – the healers –, especially those who used incantations, since these were regarded as prayers to the devil. For his zeal in persecuting those presumed guilty of practising native beliefs, Hernando Ruiz de Alarcon, a local priest born in Taxco, Guerrero (and brother of the famous playwright Juan Ruiz de Alarcon) was appointed an ecclesiastical judge and assigned the task of surveying the persistence of these old customs and beliefs. The result was the *Treatise on the Heathen Superstitions That Today Live Among the Indians Native to This New Spain*, published in 1629.

The *Treatise* is one of the most important sources dealing with native religion, beliefs and medicine for early colonial Mexico and has attracted many scholars (Lopez Austin 1966, 1967, 1969, 1970, 1975; Garibay 1958; Gruzinski 1988). Although Ruiz de Alarcon is regarded as a flawed ethnographer because of his obvious biases against native traditions, the accounts and invocations recorded in the document provide information about cosmology, concepts of deities and their interactions with humans, and ideas about health and sickness. Between Sahagun's *Florentine Codex* and the *Treatise* we can note a shift in the indigenous rituals because of the adoption of Christian images and symbols. However, the underlying structure revealed in this document continues to be that of the indigenous religion (Gruzinski 1988; Andrews and Hassig 1984).

> . . . I have arrested and punished many Indian men and women for this crime (healing with invocations to Mesoamerican deities and fortune telling) although, having made a calculation, there have been more women than men . . . (They) are found in many provinces, because, on account of the name of seers, they are highly respected and regarded and very well provided with necessities . . . (*Treatise,* translation, Andrews and Hassig 1984).

Of the thirty or so healers mentioned by Ruiz de Alarcon, around twenty were women. The portrait that emerges is of women with authority who were staunch, resolute and wise. It suggests that just as the old religious beliefs persisted, the presence of powerful women healers may have likewise been a reflection of women's healing functions before the conquest. Gruzinski comments: ' . . . One would hardly exaggerate these women's importance, who participate on equal footing with men, in the transmission of ancient cultures. Besides, it is not the first time that we see them intervene so manifestly in the process of acculturation and counter acculturation . . . ' After analysing the social context of those women healers, he adds: ' . . . It seems that their function has little to do with social origin, age (some are old but not all) or condition (widows, married women) and only one knows how to read and write . . . ' (Gruzinski 1988). Some healers achieved great prestige and notoriety and even outwitted the clergy's efforts to find them. Ruiz de Alarcon tells of the case of the

. . . old woman Isabel Maria, an inhabitant of Temimilzinco who uses spells and incantations, I took measures to get my hands on her. And she was so careful that for more than one year I was not able to discover her . . . this old woman was so pleased with the strength of this false incantation, that she said she had unburdened her conscience with having made it known and not hiding any of the things that God had communicated to her for the benefit of man . . . (*Treatise*, trans. Andrews and Hassig 1984).

Ruiz de Alarcon also speaks of a woman with a considerable reputation among the indigenous populations of Guerrero and Morelos:

. . . In the village of Iguala (in Guerrero) . . . I arrested an Indian woman called Mariana, a seer, a liar, a healer, of the type called 'Ticitl'. This Mariana declared that what she knew and used in her sorcery and frauds she had learned from another Indian woman, Mariana's sister, and that the sister had not learned it from another person, but that it had been revealed to her, because when the sister was consulting the *ololiuhqui** about the cure of an old wound, having become intoxicated with the strength of the drink, she summoned the sick person and blew upon the wound some embers, where upon the wound healed immediately.' The account goes on to relate how 'a youth whom she judged to be an angel' appeared to her and consoled her, telling her that God was granting her a favour. She would be able to cure wounds and diseases and thereby support herself even though she lived in 'poverty and much misery'. The youth put her on a cross and taught her the ways she knew for curing 'which were seven or more exorcisms and invocations' . . . (ibid).

IV. Rituals of healing

It should be clear from the accounts in the *Treatise* that religious ritual was essential to healing. Today it remains true that more than administering a plant for a disease, almost all the women herbalists, bone-setters and other healers carry out rituals. They may be simple prayers or invocations, or they may be long and complex, but they involve the *curandera* in an encounter with divine power. For them, illness cannot be reduced to a simple imbalance susceptible of being restored by taking the correct chemical substance. It is in this dimension that the power of women

*The seeds of this plant are used to prepare a drink that produces an altered state of consciousness.

healers is most evident. The ability to drive out bad airs (spirits) from their patients, neutralize the evil eye, go in search of a lost 'tonalli' (life force), free patients from mischievous or evil spirit entities depends on their capacity to act in the realm of the spirit. As Jacinto Arias, an indigenous anthropologist, points out:

> . . . Traditional doctors, those which we call 'iloletik', have as the centre of their healing action the spirit, the soul, and not the plants or other kind of material medicine. This is why they read pulses and use other methods to diagnose social causes of sickness rather than physical or physiological causes . . . (C)ertain medicinal plants are used as a support but these are not the core of their actions (Herrasti and Ortiz 1986).

Elena Islas speaks of the method used by her mother Doña Rufina to heal in San Miguel Tzinacapan, in the sierra of Puebla:

> My mother cured everything: fright, bad airs, evil eye . . . She cured everything but she never did any evil, even though she knew how to do it. She had to pray all day. Only if she went out or if people came to visit her did she stop . . . she prayed till midnight (Almeida 1986).

In order to show different styles of ritual healing practised by contemporary curanderas in Mexico, I have chosen descriptions from various studies and from my own notes made as an observer-participant in healing ceremonies. The first is an account of a healing ritual performed by an Indian woman which shows strong pre-Columbian influence.

Doña Lucía

It is just after dawn in the simple house of a peasant woman, Doña Lucía, who stands before a Mexican woman from the city. On the floor a black pottery incense burner of pre-Columbian design sends up a steady stream of incense. Both patient and healer are fasting. She has previously diagnosed her patient as suffering from an illness brought on by the jealousy and harmful thoughts of her co-workers. Doña Lucía looks toward her altar with its many holy pictures and statues of Jesus, Mary and the saints. She invokes the divine presence asking God to take away the perturbances that afflict the woman. Picking up the burner, she fans the incense to every part of the woman's body. Then she gives her a packet of finely chopped plant root and tells her how to take it. It will purge her, Doña Lucía explains, but after that she will begin to get better. Before setting out for home, the woman leaves a donation on the altar.

Similar healing acts have been carried out for centuries in Mexico by women and are an extension of their abilities and position in the community and likewise reflect the position of the feminine in their cosmology.

Spiritualism

Marian Trinitary Spiritualism is a popular – mainly urban – religion which is expanding rapidly throughout Mexico and into Central and South America. According to some researchers, the movement began in 1866 with Roque Rojas, an ex-seminarian, in the town of Contreras outside Mexico City (Ortiz 1979). Within its beliefs and rituals can be found traces of pre-Hispanic, Christian, Hindu and Judaic elements. Followers refer to themselves as the Lost Tribes of Israel; they believe in reincarnation; they address a divinity in their chants who is present in oceans, rivers, stones, light, insects and earth. The image of the Trinity (God the Father, the Son and Holy Spirit) is the central piece of the altar.

In spiritualism, curing is accomplished through 'spiritual' techniques. Some herbs are administered (this varies from chapter to chapter) and massage is often used, but healing takes place by the action of the spirit protectors working through the healer who is in a trance state. Spiritualism encourages direct relationship with the world of spirit protectors. In spiritualist temples the same levels in the hierarchy are open to men and women, and often women hold the highest positions (Finkler 1976; Lagarriga 1976; Ortiz 1989).

Dõna Lola was a leader and founder of the spiritualist temple in Cuernavaca, Morelos. She selected and trained members who had 'faculties'. Through trances and spirit possession, a woman becomes a bearer of knowledge and acquires special dignity. Transformed into the receptacle of the divine, she guides, cures and teaches.

Currently the spiritualists have seven chapters or 'seals', each with its own characteristics. The Sixth Seal was founded by Damiana Oveido, whose biography was converted into a founding myth and begins as follows:

The first woman who descended to the planet earth in order to make the light of the Lord known was Damiana Oviedo. Since her birth she predicted many things that the Lord had indicated . . .

According to her biography she only lived three days after birth then died and:
was brought back to life twenty-four hours later and led a normal life . . . At thirteen years of age she went to Manzanillo and there

founded the first temple . . . and the Lord spoke with her and told her that she should plant the light in Mexico and she went there and founded a temple and many followed her (Lagarriga 1976).

Another style of healing involves establishing an altered state of consciousness in order to diagnose and cure. In San Bartolo Yautepec, a Zapotec village in the state of Oaxaca, a study recounts the use of the *ololiuhqui* seed (see Ruiz de Alarcon above) by the healer Paula Jimenez. A drink is prepared in a ritual that requires precise handling of the seeds, chanting, invocations and awareness of proper time and place. The potion, in different quantities, is drunk by the *curandera* and patient. The healer, now with access to divine knowledge and power, can facilitate the cure (Wasson 1966).

In yet another style of ritual healing, we find 'Sister' Julia, as she is called by the residents of her poor urban neighbourhood in Cuernavaca. During a ceremony to cure a small girl of a potentially fatal scorpion bite, she talks to an image of Jesus. He is there healing through her as she acts out giving an injection to the girl. She speaks informally to the image, even harshly when the girl at first does not improve. The divinity she calls on is not a transcendent being but an immanent one. The image she addresses is the crucified Christ. The cure is accomplished through her power to call on divine aid (Baytelman 1980).

Conclusion

Ritual healing in Mexico has been practised since pre-Hispanic times. As healers, women transcend the limitations of their social and cultural roles. Ethnographic evidence indicates that in Mexico women were in the majority as healers. This is true today among the spiritualists, for example, where they predominate in the temple hierarchy. The numerical predominance is also qualitative. The maximum authority among the '*graniceros*' (a type of *curandero* who controls rain, hail and lightning) in the volcano region near Mexico City is a woman and the position is handed down through female lineage (Viesca 1984).

In the ancient Meso-American cosmos and in popular healing practices where its influence still pervades, medicine is the art of exchange with the divine. It is the capacity for immersion in divinity and mastery over revealed information. It is the skill to illuminate hidden mysteries and the power to intervene in uncertain destinies and order them in harmony. Women in Mexico participate in healing rituals according to their skills in answer to the needs of those around them.

English version with Jacqueline Mosio

References

G. Aguirre Beltran, *Medicina y Magia*, Mexico 1980

E. Almeida, et al., *Psicología au~tóctona mexicana: Doña Rufina Manzano Ramirez de San Miguel Tzinacapan*, Puebla (Ms 1986)

Roger Bastide, *The African Religions of Brazil*, London 1978

B. Baytelman, *Etnobotánica en el Estado de Morelos*, Mexico 1980

G. Bonfil, 'Lo propio y lo ajeno', in *La Cultura Popular*, ed. A. Colombres, Mexico 1984

Kaja Finkler, *Spiritualist Healers in Mexico*, Amherst 1985

J. Galinier, 'Cosmología e interpretación de la enfermedad', *México Indígena* 9, March-April 1986

Angel Garibay, 'Semejanza de algunos conceptos filosóficos de las culturas hindú y náhuatl', in *Cuadernos del Seminario de problemas científicos y filosóficos*, No. 15, Second Series, 1959

S. Gruzinski, *La Colonización de L'Imaginaire*, Paris 1988

L. and A. Ortiz Herrasti, 'Medicina del alma: entrevista a Jacinto Arias', *Mexico Indígeno* 9, March-April 1986

Eva Hunt, *The Transformation of the Hummingbird*, 1977

A. Isabel Lagarriga, *Medicina Tradicional y Espiritismo*, Mexico, Sep-Setentas No. 191, 1975

Diego Landa, *Relación de las Cosas de Yucatán*, Introduction by Angel M. Garibay, Mexico 1960

B. Las Casas, *Apologética historia*, Mexico 1967

M. Leon Portilla, *La filosofía náhuatl*, Mexico 1963.

A. Lopez Austin, *Cuerpo humano e ideología: Las concepciones de los antiguos Nahuas*, Vol. II, Mexico 1984

S. Marcos, 'Cognitive Structures and Medicine: The Challenge of Popular Medicines', CURARE, Vol. II, 1988, 87–96

– (a) 'Curas, diosas y erotismo: El catolicismo frente a los Indios', in *Mujeres e iglesia, sexualidad y aborto en América Latina*, ed. A. Portugal, Mexico 1989

– (b) 'Mujeres, cosmovisión y medicina: Las curanderas mexicanas', in *Trabajo, poder y sexualidad*, ed. O. Oliveira, Mexico 1989

S. Ortiz, 'Origen, desarrollo y características del espiritualismo en México', *América Indígena*, Vol. XXXIX, No.1, Jan-March 1979; 'El poder del trance o la participación feminina en el Espiritualismo Trinitario Mariano', in *Cuadernos de Trabajo DEAS*, Mexico 1979

H. Ruiz de Alarcon, *Treatise on the Heathen Superstitions that Today Live Among the Indian Natives to This New Spain* (1629), Trans. and ed. by J. Richard Andrews and Ross Hassig, Norman, Oklahoma 1984

F.B. Sahagun, *Historia General de las Cosas de Nueva España (1577) Florentine Codex*, trans. by Dibble and Anderson 1969

Eric Thompson, *Historia y religión de los mayas*, Mexico 1975

Victor Turner, *Image and Pilgrimage in Christian Culture*, New York 1978

Carlos Viesca, 'El Medico Mexica', in *Historia General de la Medicina en México*, Tomo I, *Mexico Antiguo*, Mexico 1984

E. Vogt, *Tortillas for the Gods*, Cambridge, Mass. 1976

G. Wasson, 'Ololiuhqui and Other Hallucinogens of Mexico', in *Summa antropológica en homenaje a Roberto J. Weitlaner*, Mexico City 1966

Contributors

DAVID POWER was born in Dublin, Ireland, in 1932. A member of the Oblates of Mary Immaculate, he was ordained priest in 1956 and holds a doctorate in theology from the Liturgical Institute of San Anselmo, Rome. Having taught in Ireland and at the Gregorian University, Rome, he is currently professor of systematic theology and liturgy at the Catholic University of America, Washington, DC (USA). He has been one of the editorial directors of *Concilium* since 1970. His latest book publications are *The Sacrifice We Offer. The Tridentine Dogma And Its Reinterpretation*, Edinburgh 1987, and *Liturgy and Culture*, Washington, DC 1991.

MARY COLLINS, OSB, a co-director of *Concilium*, is director of the Liturgical Studies Program and chairperson of the Department of Religion and Religious Education in the School of Religious Studies at The Catholic University of America in Washington, DC. She is the author of *Worship: Renewal to Practice* and *Women at Prayer*, as well as numerous articles in *Worship, The Jurist*, and *La Vie spirituelle*.

PATRICIA S. MALOOF is a medical anthropologist with a specialization in maternal/child health and the Middle East. She is currently the education and training coordinator at Connections Intercultural Human Services, a component of Catholic Charities of Richmond, Virginia (USA). For the last ten years, she has worked in the US with refugees and immigrants in the areas of health, education, employment and counselling. Dr Maloof speaks Farsi and French and is assistant professorial lecturer in Anthropology at the Catholic University of America and George Washington University, Washington, DC.

DIONISIO BOROBIO was born in Spain in 1938 and ordained in Bilbao in 1965. He studied at the Gregorian and the Anselmo Liturgical Institute in Rome, and holds a degree in philosophy from the Complutense University of Madrid, as well as a doctorate in liturgical theology. He lectures on liturgy and the sacraments at the Pontifical University of Salamanca. Besides numerous articles, his main published works are *Confirmar hoy. De la teología a la praxis* (1974), *La doctrina penitencial en el Liber Orationum Psalmographus* (1977), *La penitencia en la Iglesia hispánica del s. IV–VII (1978), Proyecto de iniciación cristiana* (1980), *Ministerio sacerdotal. Ministerios laicales* (1982) and *Sacramentos en comunidad* (1985).

BASILIUS GROEN was born in 1953. He studied theology and modern Greek in Nijmegen, Amsterdam, Trier and Thessaloniki. He is working at the Institute for Eastern Christianity in Nijmegen.

MEINRAD HEBGA was born in Cameroun in 1931. He studied theology at the Gregorian University in Rome and philosophy and psychology at the Sorbonne, where he also gained his doctorate. He was missionary professor of anthropology and theology at Loyola University, Chicago and Harvard, in 1975–76 and at the Gregorian from 1977; for a number of years he has been professor at the Catholic Institute of West Africa, Abidjan. He is researching into sorcery and exercising a ministry of healing by prayer in many African countries. In addition to many articles, his publications include *Les Étapes des Regroupements africains*, Dakar 1968; *Croyance et Guérison*, Yaoundé 1973; *Émancipation d'Églises sous tutelle*, Paris 1976; *Dépassements*, Paris 1977; *Sorcellerie, Chimère dangereuse?*, Abidjan 1979; *Sorcellerie et Prière de délivrance*, Paris 1982.

ADOLPHE RAZAFINTSALAMA was born in 1926; at present he is Professor of Social and Religious Anthropology at the Higher Institute of Theology at Tananarive, Madagascar, and also at Tananarive University. He is also president of the Ecumenical Church Office. He has recently written an *Ecumenical Guide for the Catholic Church* (in Malagasy) which is about to be published and a number of articles in the Zaire Jesuit journal *Telema*.

MEREDITH B. McGUIRE is Professor of Sociology and Anthropology at Trinity University in San Antonio, Texas. He is Past-President of the Society for the Scientific Study of Religion and the Association for the Sociology of Religion. He has written numerous articles in the sociology of religion and in medical sociology/anthropology; his books include *Religion: The Social Context, Pentecostal Catholics, Ritual Healing in Suburban America*, and *Health, Illness and the Social Body*.

SYLVIA MARCOS is a Mexican women's rights activist who lives in Cuernavaca. She is a member of Catholics for a Free Choice and has lectured widely in the US. Her present positions are: Director of the

Center for Psychoethnological Research, Cuernavaca; Research Associate in Medical Anthropology for DEAS-INAH (Instituto Nacional de Antropología e Historia); Research Associate for PIEM (Programa Interdisciplinario de Estudios de la Mujer), Colegio de Mexico; she has a private practice as a psychotherapist. Her publications include: *Manicomios y Prisiones*. Mexico 1983, [2]1987; *Alternativas a La Psiquiatría, Dossier Mexico*, Mexico 1982, [2] 1986; *Antipsiquiatría y Política*, Mexico 1980, [3]1989.

Members of the Advisory Committee for Liturgy

Directors

Mary Collins OSB	Washington, DC	USA
David Power OML	Washington, DC	USA

Members

Ad Blijlevens CSsR	Heerlen	The Netherlands
Boris Bobrinskoy	Boulogne	France
Londi Boka di Mpasi SJ	Kinshasa-Gombe	Zaire
Anscar Chupungco OSB	Rome	Italy
Irénée-Henri Dalmais OP	Paris	France
Luigi Della Torre	Rome	Italy
Michel Dujarier	Ouidah	Bénin
Joseph Gelineau SJ	Moret sur Loing	France
Maucyr Gibin SSS	Sao Paulo, SP	Brazil
Kathleen Hughes RSCJ	Chicago, IL,	USA
Denis Hurley OMI	Durban	South Africa
Aidan Kavanagh OSB	New Haven, Conn.	USA
Guy Lapointe OP	Montreal	Canada
Juan Llopis	Barcelona	Spain
Gerard Lukken	Tilburg	The Netherlands
Luis Maldonado	Madrid	Spain
Paul Puthanangady SDB	Bangalore	India
Gail Ramshaw	Philadelphia, PA	USA
Heinrich Rennings	Paderborn	West Germany
Philippe Rouillard OSB	Rome	Italy
Anton Scheer	Rosmalen	The Netherlands
Kevin Seasoltz OSB	Washington, DC	USA
Robert Taft SJ	Rome	Italy
Evangelista Vilanova OSB	Montserrat	Spain
Geoffrey Wainwright	Durham, NC	USA

Members of the Board of Directors

Back issues still available

1990 issues: £4.00 each - whole year (all six issues) £20.00
1   On the Threshold of the Third Millennium
2   The Ethics of World Religions and Human Rights
3   Asking and Thanking
4   Collegiality put to the Test
5   Coping with Failure
6   1492-1992 The Voice of the Victims

Other back numbers are available as follows:

Issues at £1.00 each

1965
1   Dogma *ed. Schillebeeckx: The very first issue*
2   Liturgy *On the Vatican Constitution: Jungmann and Gelineau*
3   Pastoral *ed. Rahner: The first issue on this topic*
4   Ecumenism *Kung on charismatic structure, Baum on other churches*
5   Moral Theology *Its nature: law, decalogue, birth control*
6   Church and World *Metz, von Balthasar, Rahner on ideology*
7   Church History *Early church, Constance, Trent, religious freedom*
8   Canon Law *Conferences and collegiality*
9   Spirituality *Murray Rogers, von Balthasar: East and West*
10 Scripture *Inspiration and Authority; R.E. Murphy, Bruce Vawter*
1966
11 Dogma *Christology - Congar, Schoonenberg, Vorgrimler*
12 Liturgy *The liturgical assembly, new church music*
13 Pastoral *Mission after Vatican 2*
14 Ecumenism *Getting to know the other churches*
15 Moral Theology *Religious freedom - Roland Bainton, Yves Congar*
16 Church and World *Christian faith v. atheism - Moltmann, Ricoeur*
17 Church History *Jansenism, Luther, Gregorian Reform*
18 Religious Freedom *In Judaism, Hinduism, Spain, Africa*
19 Religionless Christianity? *Bernard Cooke, Duquoc, Geffre*
20 Bible and Tradition *Blenkinsopp, Fitzmeyer, P. Grelot*
1967
21 Revelation and Dogma *A reconsideration*
23 Atheism and Indifference *Includes two Rahner articles*
24 Debate on the Sacraments *Thurian, Kasper, Ratzinger, Meyendorff*
25 Morality, Progress and History *Can the moral law develop?*
26 Evolution *Harvey Cox, Ellul, Rahner, Eric Mascall*
27 Church History *Sherwin-White and Oberman - Enlightenment*
28 Canon Law - Theology and Renewal *Hopes for the new Canon Law*
29 Spirituality and Politics *Balthasar; J.A.T. Robinson discussed*
30 The Value of the OT *John McKenzie, Munoz Iglesias, Coppens*